Abram Midani
New york 1960

D1260800

STAR MAKER

By HOMER CROY

Books Made into Motion Pictures

WEST OF THE WATER TOWER

THEY HAD TO SEE PARIS
   (Will Rogers' first talking picture)

DOWN TO EARTH
   (Will Rogers as star)

SIXTEEN HANDS
   (made into a motion picture under the title
   I'm from Missouri)

LADY TUBBS
   (Alice Brady as star)

FAMILY HONEYMOON

STAR MAKER

The Story of D. W. Griffith

by HOMER CROY

Introduction by MARY PICKFORD

DUELL, SLOAN AND PEARCE
New York

Croy, Homer, 1883– Star maker; the story of D. W. Griffith. Introd. by
Mary Pickford. [1st ed.] New York, Duell, Sloan and Pearce [1959]
210 p. illus. 21 cm. 1. Griffith, David Wark, 1875–1948. 1. Title.
PN1998.A3G73 927.92 59–6691 ‡ Library of Congress

First edition

Thanks are due to Harper & Brothers for permission to quote a passage
from *Tallulah, My Autobiography*, by Tallulah Bankhead. Copyright,
1952, by Tallulah Bankhead.

MANUFACTURED IN THE UNITED STATES OF AMERICA

VAN REES PRESS • NEW YORK

CONTENTS

ILLUSTRATIONS

following page 50

"Mr. D. W." as an actor

Young Ben Alexander with Griffith

Mary Pickford

Douglas Fairbanks, Mary Pickford, Charlie Chaplin, and Griffith

Griffith the director

Mae Marsh in *The Birth of a Nation*

The Reverend Thomas E. Dixon

Henry B. Walthall

Lillian Gish in *The Birth of a Nation*

Linda Arvidson in *As the Candle Burns*

Carol Dempster and W. C. Fields

Griffith at his second wedding

Griffith and his bride

The family tomb

The house Griffith bought for his mother

FOREWORD

I AM PLEASED THAT I CAN PASS ALONG TO THE reading public the first story of the life of David Wark Griffith. He lived in a blaze of publicity for his stars and his stories, but he told little of himself, especially of his early life; nothing of his personal life. He had a secret marriage; he spoke not at all of this. In fact most people thought he was a bachelor. And, in one sense, he was.

I met him only once. I spent an evening with him when he was just starting to make *The Birth of a Nation*. I was representing *Leslie's Weekly;* no wonder he gave me so much time, for it was for this magazine that he had written his one published poem—"The Wild Duck." He didn't mention the poem, but I expect during the evening he thought of it many times. Strangely enough, I cannot remember one important thing he said; and the piece I wrote is so inane that I hope no human eye ever falls on it again. I certainly did not realize that he would become a world figure, and that someday I would be attempting to tell his story. And I don't think he had the faintest idea then that he would become a world figure, especially in a medium that later he came to despise.

I have had access to his autobiography which is still in manuscript form. It deals with his early days, for he never finished it. It does, however, give some vivid pictures of his life as a farm boy.

The intimate material in this book has come from people who knew him. He was strangely uncommunicative about himself. As an example, when he first came to New York he couldn't land a job as an actor, so he got one working in the subway that was being built; his special assignment was wielding a pick and shovel. He told his brother Albert L. Griffith about this, but mentioned it only once. And he told Evelyn Griffith, and one or two others. That was all.

He made eighteen stars:

Mary Pickford
Lillian Gish
Dorothy Gish
Mae Marsh
Blanche Sweet
Richard Barthelmess
Henry B. Walthall
Robert Harron
Florence Lawrence

Mabel Normand
Miriam Cooper
Carol Dempster
Una Merkel
James Kirkwood
Owen Moore
Joseph Schildkraut
Monte Blue
Louis Wolheim

He launched, or furthered, the film careers of:

Lionel Barrymore
Noel Coward
Douglas Fairbanks
DeWolf Hopper
Erich von Stroheim
Carmel Myers
William Boyd
    (Hopalong Cassidy)
Sir Herbert Beerbohm-Tree
Lupe Velez
Colleen Moore

Constance Talmadge
Ruth St. Denis
Mack Sennett
Ralph Graves
Ivan Lebedeff
W. C. Fields
Zita Johann
Ivor Novello
Bessie Love
Alma Rubens

I want to thank his family (I've gone into detail on the last page) and I want to thank his widow, Mrs. D. W. Griffith, who lives in New York. And I want to thank Lillian Gish, Dorothy Gish, Mary Pickford, Anita Loos, Mae Marsh, Richard Barthelmess . . . the latter dodged me for three months before I nailed him. And I want to thank Richard Griffith (no relation), curator of the Film Library of the New York Museum of Modern Art. And I'll be dogged, if he didn't jump up and run off to Brazil, just as I started to pump him. I had to wait seven weeks, but I got him.

And I want to thank the people on the Louisville, Kentucky, *Courier-Journal* who told me where to spade, especially Boyd Martin, who knew Griffith for thirty years; and James S. Pope, who knew him for ten. And those mint juleps in Louisville. I've never had one before on its native heath. I want to thank them. I am now speaking of the juleps.

I don't seem to be doing a very good job of thanking people and giving credits, but I thank them in my heart, and say again I'm glad I can set down this brief history of a great man and a tragic figure.

Personal: I'd like to add that I had something to do with the early days of motion pictures and knew a bit of their history. In 1914 I made a trip around the world for Universal, making travel films. In those days travel pictures had little appeal, so the ones I made were released as half-reel subjects, under the name Joker Comedies, of all things. But that was the way things were done in those days. I was in China when the war broke out. Later, I traveled through India making motion pictures of the war preparations (no censor then).

In 1915, when I was married, Universal News Reel (edited by Jack Cohn) made pictures of our wedding. Ours was the first wedding ever shown on the screen. (I've still got her.)

In 1918, I wrote the first book on the making of motion pictures: *How Motion Pictures Are Made.* The other day, when I was getting ready to write this foreword, I reread the book. I was shocked. The book was as out-of-date as a whipsocket.

During the First World War, I was a civilian attached to the Signal Corps as a motion-picture expert. I was in the Pathé Laboratory outside of Paris. I knew little or nothing about motion pictures, but this wasn't too embarrassing, for no one knew much either about combat pictures or about pictures of training or service of supplies.

I suppose all this drew me to attempt a life of the Great Film Pioneer.

—THE AUTHOR

INTRODUCTION

By Mary Pickford

WHEN I MET THE FABULOUS DAVID WARK
Griffith I was far from being awed. Truthfully, I held not
only him but everyone else connected with the despised
"flickers" in complete contempt.

Perhaps this insufferable attitude could be partially explained by the fact that I lacked but a few days of my fifteenth
birthday. As you may imagine, I have had my well deserved
comeuppance since—and trust that I now view the world with
more tolerant eyes and, above all, give full credit to the great
genius of D. W. Griffith. I am only one of many whom he
sponsored and who owe him profound gratitude. He developed innumerable revolutionary ideas that changed the entire
movie-making technique—many of which are still being used
today. It would take not just one but many volumes, as I see
it, to recount his brilliant contributions adequately.

He asked me exactly what experience I had had in the
theater and I replied haughtily, "Only ten years, sir!" He said,
"You don't look that old—but I think I will introduce you to
the camera," and he did.

From that moment on I was to learn that this extraordinary
man had been chosen to usher into the world a new medium
that would give world-wide entertainment and exert a tremendous and exciting influence upon the world's thinking and
habits. This new medium developed into a great ambassador

for our Uncle Sam and a truly far-reaching salesman of our American way of life.

I see D. W. now, standing beside the camera, a lean, hawk-like individual with an old straw hat, the top unraveled (he believed the sun would stop him from losing his hair). He wore a large, black, Chinese prayer ring, which he constantly twirled while directing us, and at the same time he jingled silver coins in his trouser pocket. Eccentric? Yes. But certainly no poseur. D. W.'s presence was magnetic. Nothing before or since has given me the warm satisfaction of a performance that pleased Mr. Griffith.

You may ask, "Did you have fun?" Of course we did. But we were all young and full of the zest of life and creation. We had our tragedies, especially when our performances did not measure up to what was expected of us. Then, too, there was keen rivalry and jealousy over the plum roles we felt would advance us artistically.

Mr. Griffith kept us on the *qui vive* by pitting our talents and temperament one against the other. As I look back along the many years, I realize that David Wark Griffith was a great virtuoso who played on the heartstrings of his actors. No one during my entire career ever reached me, mentally or emotionally, as he did. Sometimes he would say while directing me, "Pickford, you read my thoughts," and I believe I actually did.

It was a great sadness to me and all those who knew and loved him and respected his tremendous contribution to the motion-picture industry, that Mr. Griffith, during the latter part of his life, was so neglected and so tragically ignored by the industry that he greatly helped to create. But I recall that he was an extremely sensitive and proud Kentuckian who would not for an instant tolerate anything that he thought even remotely resembled condescension on the part of others.

Were it possible to roll back the years it would be a joyous moment to hear that sonorous voice call out, "Bitzer—camera— Pickford—enter, and remember not to take up too much film in doing what you rehearsed. Film footage costs money."

But perhaps where he and the beloved Billy Bitzer are now, they have that big Biograph camera greatly improved and are preparing stunts for the old Biographers when we arrive over there. I devoutly hope so.

Sentimental? Why not?

STAR MAKER

CHAPTER 1

BORN ON A FARM SEVENTEEN MILES FROM LOUISVILLE, KENTUCKY

DAVID WARK GRIFFITH WAS TALL AND THIN, with a large, bony nose, which he tried to make less noticeable by wearing a wide-brimmed floppy hat. He wore the hat almost constantly, indoors and out, this so that his nose would not be so conspicuous. If someone mentioned his nose, he would call it his "Duke of Wellington" nose. In addition, he had an unusually wide mouth and a long, narrow chin. It all added up to make him a striking-looking man.

He looked upon himself as an aristocrat. His family had been plantation and slave owners. His mother's people—the Oglesbys —were an important family.

His father was a colonel in the War Between the States and was known as "Roaring Jake," a large man who got the name from the way he bellowed out his commands. Once he was leading the First Kentucky Cavalry near Charleston, Tennessee, when he was shot off his horse and was wounded so badly that he could not get back on again. A man with a horse and buggy started to dash past, wanting to get out of the business as fast as he could. Colonel Griffith drew his pistol and ordered the man to get out and help him in, which the man had sense enough to do. Then, picking up the lines, Colonel Griffith led a cavalry charge—the first time in history an officer ever led his men in a charge in a buggy. The son was very proud of this and had it chiseled on his father's tombstone, and there it is today in the Mount Tabor Methodist graveyard, in the community known as Crestwood, seventeen miles from Louisville, Kentucky, where young David was born on January 22, 1875.

There were, in all, eight children. David was the next to youngest. Rearing eight children, after the destruction brought about by the Civil War, was a problem. Albert L. Griffith was the youngest, and he, as I write, is still living, and to him I owe much for rebuilding those early days.

The father loved Shakespeare and liked to put on "readings." This he did at the schoolhouse, at the church, and in his own home. There he would stand—this big-bodied man—delivering Shakespeare. Young David was tremendously impressed by these recitals; and he was tremendously impressed by his father.

The story of the family, after the war, was like that of thousands of others in the South. Before the War Between the States it had been a prosperous family. After the war, it was impoverished. The family had had slaves, and again, like a tale of the old South, the slaves faithfully remained with the family. Another bit of similarity to the accepted tale of the South—young David had a "mammy" to take care of him.

A southern gentleman did not work in the fields. And this the old colonel never did; he "bossed" the colored help. But now there was no colored help; the family was so poor that the former slaves had to strike out for themselves. On top of this, the old colonel had other troubles. His war wounds grew worse. He was elected to the Kentucky legislature but could not attend all the sessions because of his wounds. Finally he was confined to his home. Young David—he was never called Davey—would sit beside the chair where his father was propped among the cushions, and listen to his father read. His father no longer could put his great fervor and passion into the readings. Sometimes his voice would trail off.

When the boy was ten years old his father died. David did not become the head of the family, but he did become the head dreamer. The family said he was "impractical." He could never quite drive a nail straight; and he couldn't saw a board without the blade heading for parts unknown.

The school David attended was a part log, part sawed-board building, about sixteen feet square, with the chinks between the logs filled with hard yellow clay. The room was heated by a wood-burning stove—the children nearest it suffocating, the ones farthest away shivering. Water was carried from a well about a hundred yards away, a bucket at a time. The bucket was placed on a shelf; in the bucket was a tin dipper, used by all. When a child did not drink all he had dipped up, he poured the remainder back into the bucket.

One of the games was "Black Man." Two or three of the older and stronger children stood off all the rest. The others were put into two lines, facing each other. The leader of the two strong children would approach the line, with most of the school in it, and say, "What will you do if you see the Black Man coming?"

The others would shout, "Run right through, like a white man," and then all would try to run through to the bases, or until they were tagged. The children considered it great fun; the mothers considered it great work, what with buttons being ripped off and clothes torn.

At recess time, when the children were not playing, the boys whittled out forks for slingshots, made whistles out of slippery elm, or dolls out of acorns. The dolls had natural noses owing to the shape of the acorns, a slit for a mouth, and tiny beads for eyes. When a boy had an acorn doll nicely fashioned, he would give it to his girl.

Reading and elocution were the subjects stressed; much time was spent on what was called "articulation, inflection, and emphasis." The last Friday afternoon of every month the parents came in to attend "the exercises." This was little David's chance; he liked to "recite," and this he did, loud and confidently. A poem that was recited again and again by the "scholars" was "The Ballad of the Tempest," which went:

> And as thus we sat in darkness,
> Each one busy in his prayers,
> "We are lost," the Captain shouted
> As he staggered down the stairs.
>
> But his little daughter whispered
> As she took his icy hand,
> "Isn't God upon the ocean
> Just the same as on the land?"

Once young David recited this with such great feeling that one of the visiting women wept openly. The boy was, for a time, the school hero.

One morning, as he was walking across the fields to school, he came to the creek the banks of which were lined with willows. There had been a sleet storm the night before, and the limbs of the willows were bent down; the morning sun was shining on them and giving off reflections. He stopped to admire the shimmering spectacle. As he did so, he was shaken through and through, for there was the face of Christ. He stood transfixed, held by something bigger than himself. Why should Christ suddenly show himself to him, a lone boy? Was it a sign? He started on again, plodding his way across the fields. So deep, so personal, so moving was the experience that he mentioned it to no one.

It was not long before the boy had mastered all that the school could offer. His real education was conducted by his sister Mattie, who was a better teacher than any who had served at the country school. It soon developed that the boy liked "stories"—the novels of Thackeray and Sir Walter Scott and Dickens. And he liked American history. He liked stories of "the war"—especially when the South was shown as being trampled upon.

"Someday David will be a great man," said "Miss" Mattie. Of course, she was his sister.

David worked in the fields (as little as he could) and read with a kind of fierce passion; a new world—his dream world—floated about him.

When he was seventeen, the family gave up the ghost. The "goods" were stored in three wagons and the long trip to Louisville began. One of the wagons was in command of David—this wagon had more articles fall off and become lost along the way than either of the other two wagons. David, in the front seat, saw nothing, heard nothing, dreamed everything.

The family lived first at 121 West Chestnut Street in Louisville; they moved to 625 First Street, then to 414 East Gray Street, then to 930 Fifth Street, then to 423 West Chestnut, then to 330 West Fourth Street—each house was shabbier than the one they'd left. The family wasn't alone in this, for other families had had to pull up their roots and try to survive in new locations. There was no complaining among the members of the Griffith family; they'd get along, some way or other. Young David accepted this; he'd get along some way or other, too. He was tall and "gangling" and there was that great hump of a nose, that wide mouth, that long chin.

Work! Thought had to be given to that. A magazine called

The Western Recorder was published in Louisville by the Baptist Book Concern. The magazine had been one of his reading sources, and he took himself there as fast as he could. Yes, they needed help, they said. He was delighted. However, it turned out the job was not to write for the magazine, but to sell subscriptions and books. A little cold water, here. However, arrangements were made. A horse and buggy were provided by the company, and the young salesman started out blithely to conquer the world.

One of the books published by the company was *Should Women Speak in Mixed Assemblies?* The book said they shouldn't. The publishers told him there would be a brisk demand for this helpful book. The demand, however, turned out to be far from brisk; in fact, the book was a drug on the market. Another book was *Talks on Getting Married* by T. T. Eaton, D.D., LL.D. In spite of the words of wisdom by the learned author, the demand for this book also was exceedingly modest. It soon developed that the women wanted to speak anywhere they chose without anyone telling them whether they could or not; and they didn't seem to give a fig about marriage. This was shocking. So he had to add to his sales list the *Encyclopaedia Britannica*. He was given sample pages and sample bindings and was told to commit to memory the printed sales talk, which was guaranteed to open any pocketbook. Something was fundamentally wrong with the printed sales talk, for pocketbooks didn't open as had been promised. Up and down the hills and back roads of Jefferson and Oldham counties he went, telling farmers how the magazine would help them lead a Christian life and how the encyclopaedia would educate their children. The farmers said they didn't care whether they led a Christian life or not, and that their children had just as good a chance to get an education as they'd had, and so, after a time, young Griffith gave up and let the children root for themselves.

(*Note*: The magazine is still being published, but the book *Should Women Speak in Mixed Assemblies?* is no longer available, thus leaving the matter unsettled.)

He got a job running an elevator in the John C. Lewis Department Store. To make the elevator go, he pulled a rope. To make it stop, he gave it a tug and the elevator jarred to a clanking standstill. While waiting for customers he read. He had a stool to sit on; when customers came, he stood up, turned his book face down on the stool, and gave the damned rope a yank.

At night, when he went home, he read poetry. He especially loved Browning and *Leaves of Grass*. And then, alone in his room, he began to write poetry. It can be seen he was headed for no good end.

Deep in him was this desire to write. He would tell of the great injustices in the world. He would tell the truth about the Civil War. He would show how the South had been wronged.

He did not get into high school, but this gave him no sense of inferiority. He had read more than any other boy he met; indeed, he looked down on the other boys of his age. His confidence in himself was supreme. He was a genius. He would accomplish great things. He was that young.

One day a reporter came to the store to bag a bit of news. David was fascinated. It would be wonderful if he could earn money by going around and asking questions. He waited till the reporter started out, then shyly edged up to him.

"Do you think I could get a job on the paper writing things?" he asked.

"You might," said the man, amused by the boy's earnestness.

"I'll tell you the man to see." He wrote a name. "You ask for him."

The boy was in an ecstasy of delight. A reporter! Paid to write!

He applied for and, what is more surprising, got the job. He was to pick up bits at police headquarters, bits the real reporter had overlooked. It wasn't long till the drama critic wanted somebody to help him and David was sent to the theater to write a review. A new world opened like a door. He saw Julia Marlowe in *Romola* and was carried away. If he could only write stories like this!

He spoke of his ambitions to Adolph Lestina, a member of the Meffert Stock Company; instead of laughing at him, as some people might have done, Lestina encouraged the boy. He said, "You can't write stories for the stage unless you know the stage thoroughly. Most of the great playwrights have been actors. Shakespeare was. Molière was. Dion Boucicault was." The boy looked at Lestina, deeply thankful.

He went to the manager of the company and applied for an acting job. The manager looked him over and gave him a job—thus shaking hands with History.

He was given the role of an aristocrat. To him this didn't seem out of keeping. His family were aristocrats. War had taken their money, but it hadn't taken their superiority. That was in their bones, as is marrow.

"What name do you want to use?" the manager asked.

This brought David up against the realities. He certainly didn't want to use his own, the name he was so proud of—the family which could trace itself back to early Welsh kings. One of the ancestors was Lord Brayington, who came to America with the Virginia Colony.

"David Brayington," answered the young actor-to-be like an aristocrat.

He would write his plays under his own name, but he would never act under it.

Then came the great day when David Brayington walked out on the stage, in the Temple Theatre, in Louisville, and acted. The audience took it with amazing calmness. But young David didn't. He was on his way to becoming a playwright. People would hear of him.

Daytime he ran the elevator; at night he acted. And wrote poetry. He got plays from the library and studied them as if they were lessons. But he told no one of his ambitions. This was too sacred; one never told what was deepest in him.

In *The Lights o' London* he played a comedy part; the audience took it seriously. But that was all right with David Brayington; he was learning how to put plays together. What he liked most of all was to watch how the director got certain "effects."

He was accepted as a member of the Meffert Stock Company! Oh, happy day! Lestina took him into his own dressing room, and taught him make-up, and told him things, as an actor, he could do and things to avoid. More than ever Griffith looked up to the great man.

He changed his name to Lawrence Griffith; he would save his full and proper name for his plays. The people in the company called him "Larry."

He got a job in *Ramona* by Helen Hunt Jackson. He played the part of the Indian. His interpretation gave a new insight into the American Indian.

He played any number of small parts. He knew he was not going to make a career of acting; he was only learning plays so he could, when the time came, do something more important. He continued all season with the stock company. In *Trilby* he played the clergyman—very convincingly, said the kind manager. Finally he joined the Ada Gray traveling company. That was getting up in the world—a traveling actor!—and left Louisville for the first time. He would come back to the city, famous, he promised himself. It was not long before he was with Walker Whiteside, who played mostly in the Middle West. One day, in a fit of temper, Whiteside told the boy he would never be an actor. Griffith was not too deeply hurt; he knew what he was doing.

In *The Ensign* he was asked to play the part of Abraham Lincoln. The last man in the world he wanted to play was Abe, the Abolitionist. But he did play it, and when he got into the part, he formed a grudging liking for Lincoln.

He was in a dozen plays but did not do well. He was stiff and mechanical and played every part the same. But he was doing the thing that was dearest to him: he was studying how to write plays; and when he wrote them, they would deal with mighty themes. One would deal with man and his place in the universe. He thought big thoughts—he would write big plays.

And then came an exceedingly good piece of luck. He got into Nance O'Neil's Touring Stock Company. The great Nance O'Neil! One of the plays she put on was *Elizabeth, Queen of England*. The play fascinated him; it was big, important, dramatic. That was the way he thought, he told himself. It got to Los Angeles where it opened at the Mason Opera House January 29, 1906. He played the part of Sir Francis Drake. The somewhat stunned audience said they had never dreamed Sir Francis Drake was that kind of man.

He met Linda Arvidson Johnson who was playing at the Burbank Theater in Los Angeles under the name of Linda Arvidson. She was dashing and pretty. Sir Francis Drake began to think of other things than the fate of England; in fact, he began to think of his own fate.

His play moved to San Francisco where it developed a fever and soon was sick unto death. In fact, it died. Lawrence Griffith had to get a job, and this he managed to do in the hop fields in California. It was a comedown from being Sir Francis Drake to being a hop picker.

He still believed that to be a successful playwright one first had to be an actor. He had started two plays, but they had developed fevers. He had a new idea: he'd write a story about hop picking. He had formed the habit of working in secret at night; these were his golden hours—alone with his manuscripts and his dreams. The new play told very much his own story. A young man from Kentucky met a girl in San Francisco. But the young man fell upon hard times and had to go to work in the hop fields at Ukiah to keep body and soul together. He met rugged characters who sang enchanting Mexican songs. Finally the young man raised enough money to take the girl to a night club in San Francisco rejoicing in the name of The Bull Pup. In such exciting surroundings the lovely girl could no longer rebuff the earnest young man and all was well. The hop fields would have to look after themselves.

In a fever of excitement he bundled up *A Fool and a Girl* and sent it to James K. Hackett who was thrilling audiences in *The Prisoner of Zenda*. In a few days he would hear from Mr. Hackett and Mr. Hackett would say Yes.

Good luck came and took him by the hand. He was offered a job to return to the stage and this he did, and in the play was Linda Arvidson. The play went on tour. The company was not so good as the Nance O'Neil company had been. It began to have more ups and downs than a seesaw, but finally it got to Boston and there, May 14, 1906, Linda and David were married, just as had happened so charmingly in *A Fool and a Girl*. This was fine and dandy, but the play wasn't, and, in no time at all, it failed. Linda, being an actress, thought actors were more important than writers. Sometimes the two argued about this—writer *versus* actor.

Meantime, David Griffith was writing poems and short stories which came back with the instinct of homing pigeons.

New York was the place to get an acting job, and so the two of them came to New York and began to knock at doors which remained closed as tight as bank vaults.

Then suddenly, and in a dazzle of light, something wonderful happened. *Leslie's Weekly* accepted a poem! David got a copy from the newsstand and there was the poem and there was the name he was so proud of—David Wark Griffith. He seemed to be floating, so excited, so exalted was he. He hurried to their small apartment on East Thirty-seventh Street. Some writers might have shown the poem to a wife with a casual, I-just-tossed-it-off air, but not David Griffith. It was a great, a tremendous moment, and he meant to squeeze it.

"There it is with the name I'm going to make famous."

"You mean by writing?" she asked.

"Yes—plays—important plays, not the silly girl-meets-prince plays that the stage is inflicted with. I've got something to say and I'm going to say it. I have genius and I'm not afraid to say so."

"At least you've got self-confidence."

And then he told her the thing that was deepest in him. The nights he had sat up after she had gone to bed he had been writing a play—"the play of the ages," he said. "I've decided to call it *The Treadmill*."

"Isn't that a gloomy title?"

"It shows it's a serious play and it's a title that means something. The play deals with man's progress from the time he crawled out of the primordial sea."

"There you go again, with your big words. I hope you sell it." There was a pause. "David, you're always exercising with those Indian clubs and in your underwear. It's not very appetizing. I wish you'd stop."

"I need the exercise, Linda. I'll try to pick times when you're not here."

"I wish you would, David. It gets on my nerves."

He was shocked by her casualness about his play. "I'll sell it all right. Now, Miss Linda, do you want the son of Roaring Jake to recite the poem aloud, with gestures?" he asked in his great exuberance.

"David, I want to move. Those clotheslines in the back yard depress me. When I look out, that's all I can see—ragged shirts and patched underwear till it sickens me."

"I'll be making money soon, Linda, and then off to the races! Are you ready?"

"Go ahead."

He was proud of his resonant voice—Nature might have been careless in the matter of his nose, but she had made up for her remissness by giving him a splendid, rich voice.

He read the poem with earnestness and feeling.

"How do you like it?" he asked when he finished.

"It's very interesting. You always like lamb chops and that's what I've got for you tonight. I'll put them on."

"Now I'll read it like an old-time darky would read it. Y'know, I was raised by an old colored mammy. I loved her."

He began to burlesque the poem.

In a moment she was laughing. "Do you know that I

never really knew a southerner till I met you? You're all South and I'm all San Francisco. I'm going to pull down the shade, even if it does smoke up the apartment. I just can't stand those clothes."

"Don't pay any attention to them. Think high thoughts and perform noble deeds. You want the wild duck to soar again?"

"I've heard it once."

"Remember, that wild inhabitant of the circumambient atmosphere brought us six dollars!"

"That's not much."

"Edgar Allan Poe got ten dollars for 'The Raven.' "

As she busied herself in the cramped kitchen, he sat enjoying himself, looking at the poem.

The poem appeared January 10, 1907.

> Look—how beautiful he is!
> Swift his flight as a bullet
> As he comes in from the sea in the morning.
> For the wind is from the sea in the morning.
> See! He is bound for the hilltops,
> The gold hilltops, the gold hilltops.
> There he will rest 'neath the flowers,
> The red flowers—the white and the red,
> The poppy—the flower of dreams,
> The crimson flower of dreams.
> There must be rest in the morning.
> Happy wild duck! Happy wild duck!
> For the wind is from the sea in the morning.
>
> So will he rest 'neath the roses,
> The red roses, the love roses,
> And their petals will fall around him,
> Sweet and warm around him,
> Closer and closer around him,
> Warmer and warmer around him,
> Till even in the daytime the stars shall
>   be shining.

Happy wild duck! Happy wild duck!
For the wind is from the sea in the morning.

There by the roses bloom the lilies, the
  flowers of peace,
The white flowers of peace,
Red and white together, red and white and red,
Waving and blowing together,
Blooming and waving together
On the gold hilltops in the morning,
For the wind is from the sea in the morning.

Ah me! but the wind soon changes in these
  parts,
Ah me! Ah me!
It was not so in the old days.
Look, look, ah, look, see, even now it is
  changing out, out to the sea!
Look, look, above the hilltops,
With eyes turned back to the mainland,
And tired wings wearily beating, but vainly,
For the wind blows out to sea in the
  evening.
Poor little wild duck! Poor little wild duck!
Look, there is crimson, warm on his breast!
Look, red drops fall from his breast!
Poor little wild duck! Poor little wild duck!
In the evening,
For the wind is out to the sea in the evening.

Look! He is falling, falling out to the sea.
Ah, there is mist on the sea!
There is always mist on the sea in the evening.
Perhaps his nest is beyond, I know not;
Perhaps it is built of the mist I know not,
Only with tired wings wearily beating,
And eyes turned back to the mainland,
To the red and white and red,
Waving and blowing together,
Blooming and blowing together.
He is falling out, out to the sea.

Poor little wild duck! Poor little wild duck!
In the evening when the wind blows out to the sea!
Ah me! Ah me! Ah me!
In the evening when the wind blows out to the sea.

The poem was wonderful.

CHAPTER 2

HE DIRECTS HIS FIRST PICTURE

WHY HE'D BEEN AN ACTOR TEN YEARS! HE WAS now thirty-two years old and hadn't accomplished much, he told himself. But he would! His years on the stage had taught him the fundamentals of playwriting; soon he'd sell a play. Then the two of them could give up the miserable business of acting.

Meantime, he and Linda tramped Broadway, but those grim vault doors remained closed. It was the old, old story: America was filled with touring stock companies with people not good enough to play on Broadway. There was no opening. But it wasn't completely bad, David told himself. Other actors couldn't get jobs, either; and they didn't know how to write plays. His sword had a double edge. Someday he would slash Broadway from end to end.

And then came a monstrous stroke of good fortune. James K. Hackett accepted *A Fool and a Girl*—not only that, but agreed to pay an advance of seven hundred dollars.

"We can give up acting," he cried.

"We'd better hold on," said prudent Linda. "We haven't landed jobs yet."

"We don't need jobs," said the enraptured man.

"Yes, we do. Only a few can succeed at playwriting; the stage has many jobs for actors."

So happy, so filled with promise were they that the two of

them went to the Oriental Hotel in Manhattan Beach to do nothing but enjoy the world and its blessings. But he didn't quite give up work; he pulled out a manuscript.

"This is the first real honeymoon we've had and you drag out that mess of papers."

" 'That mess of papers,' as you so euphonically call it, is going to make us rich and famous."

After a time their money began to trickle away. Back to their apartment, with the back yard filled with clothes, and again they started to trudge Broadway.

The play was to be produced in Washington with the fabulous Fanny Ward as the star—the first actress in America to have her face lifted. The darling of the headlines.

David and Linda had been living too high and too well; they did not have enough money to go to the opening. They got the Washington papers as soon as they could; the reviews were not good. One critic said the fool was the author.

They began to trudge again.

In two weeks the play closed.

But his next one wouldn't fail; this one would be the best he'd ever written.

He sent a poem to *McClure's Magazine*. Back came a letter from the great S. S. McClure himself. He liked the poem immensely and his staff liked it ... but they were loaded up on poetry and *alas!* would have to return the exquisite little poem. There was the poem, the editor's tears still damp on it.

The two continued to trudge. No doors opened. Only pocketbooks—the money going out.

They got a job in a play that was to open in Norfolk, Virginia. It failed. Back to the flapping back-yard clothes.

In Louisville there had been an in-and-out actor named Max Davidson who had gone "on the road," just as David

Griffith had done and now, like Griffith, was pounding at the doors, which opened not. The two met and David invited him to have dinner with him and Linda in their apartment. When he arrived the three soon began professional talk. Max was not feeling low, as Griffith was, and began to describe a land flowing with milk and honey. In this rich land was something that people cynically called "the flickers." Max laughed to show what he thought of such brainless people.

"There's a studio at 11 East Fourteenth Street where they make these moving pictures. They pay actors five dollars a day."

"Acting in the flickers!" said David with a shudder. "I'll never do it in the world."

"They pay cash at the end of the day."

"I wouldn't care if they paid every hour, I wouldn't demean myself by appearing in those wretched things."

"The pay is good," said Linda.

"Nobody you know, or care about, ever sees the pictures," pursued the redoubtable Max.

"But they might! I'm a stage actor and I'd rather starve than prostitute myself by appearing in Mutoscope parlors."

"Lots of stage people are slipping off and working under assumed names. Sometimes they don't even give their names. Sometimes the director goes out on the street and watches until he sees somebody who is the 'type' and braces him and offers him a job."

"I think we ought to look into it," said Linda.

"*The Great Train Robbery* has been a sensational success. It's nine hundred feet long. It has been called back to the same theater two and three times. They charge ten cents to see it."

"Ten cents!" cried the astonished man. "If that isn't robbery, I don't know what is!"

"It was directed by Edwin S. Porter, the greatest mind in the business."

"It must be exalting to be the greatest mind in flickers," said Griffith ironically.

"The story ends in a chase."

"In a chase! Can you imagine Ibsen ending a story in a chase?"

"No, I can't," Max had to admit, then said, "They buy stories. They pay fifteen dollars for a story."

"Oh!" said Griffith.

At last the evening was over. The cheerful Max was gone; David and Linda sat alone in the dingy flat.

"I think," said Linda, "we might, at least, take a look at these moving pictures."

David thought of their situation, of the increasing misfortune that was coming so brazenly to their door. "Well, all right."

They went to a small "store show."

When they came out, David said, "I can't have anything to do with such monstrosities. It almost made me sick."

"Five dollars is good pay, just now, the way things are."

"The stage has always been the thing, it always will be—not these cheap, unspeakable eye-killers."

The nickelodeon—so called because the admission was a nickel—was usually a smelly hole of a store that had been vacated and couldn't get a tenant. The seats were folding chairs hired from an undertaker. The people who patronized the shows were what was called "the great unwashed." A person with any social or financial position in the neighborhood would no more go to such a place than he would to a slaughterhouse. The showman set up a screen, put a projector in a balcony or on a platform, and let the film run into an open bag—a situation that today would start the fire department madly writing violations. The film was fragile; it had broken many times; when a break occurred, part of the film had to be snipped out in order to make the repair. As a result there were great gaps in the story and such sudden changes of scene that even the most alert members of the audience didn't know what it was all about. But that didn't matter too much; the film moved. That was the main thing. Sometimes the film broke, leaving a ghastly light on the screen. If a fly went winging by, it looked as big as a buzzard; naughty boys in the audience whooped and screamed and threw BB shot. The showman put in a piano player who kept one eye on the screen and played whatever he thought appropriate. There would be a gap in the film and he would have to leap from "Pony Boy" to "Hello, Central, Give Me Heaven."

Glass slides were inserted between films, or, sometimes, when a film broke. The slides went in for humor in a heavy way:

DON'T SPIT ON THE FLOOR.
REMEMBER THE JOHNSTOWN FLOOD.

READ THE TITLES TO YOURSELVES.
YOUR NEIGHBOR CAN PROBABLY READ.

IF YOU LIKE THIS PICTURE, TELL YOUR FRIENDS.
IF YOU DON'T, PLEASE KEEP YOUR MOUTH SHUT.

LADIES WILL TAKE OFF THEIR HATS.
WOMEN WILL LEAVE THEM ON.

LADIES DON'T SMOKE. SO WHY SHOULD YOU?

A favorite of the time was a drawing of a flirtatious young man tickling a horrified maiden under the chin. The caption read:

IF ANNOYED WHEN HERE
PLEASE TELL THE MANAGEMENT.

Glass slides also were supposed to help the audience follow the story:

THE NEXT DAY.

AN HOUR LATER.

CAME THE DAWN.

NO ONE KNEW THE SECRETS OF HER HEART.

Foolish as all this was, these films were opening up something the world had never seen in all its existence. A new art had arrived.

Griffith went a few times to "study" the kind of story that was being used. Many pictures, he found, were crude adaptations of famous stories. Well, he could do that. *La Tosca* was playing in New York. He went to the library, read the story, and wrote a short retelling of the classic and got ready to show it—not to Biograph, but to the Edison studio.

He took the Third Avenue Elevated, arrived in the Bronx, and soon was in the "studio," which consisted of three rough-looking buildings. People were coming and going in the most haphazard manner. He stopped a man who looked like a carpenter.

"I want to see Mr. Porter."

"He's over there somewhere," the man said, jerking his thumb vaguely over his shoulder.

He found Porter sitting in a small office that seemed to have been knocked together out of boards used in building sets. He had a mustache, his nose was unusually broad at the nostrils, and he was wearing a derby hat. He was an inspired mechanic. He had come to the studio as a cameraman and through ability had become a director and was now the dominant man in the studio.

"I'm a writer and a playwright, and I've written a story that might interest you."

"We're always looking for good stories," said Porter.

"I think you'll like this one."

Porter read it then and there, Griffith watching like a lynx.

Porter put down the manuscript. "I'm afraid it's not just what we want," said the cruel man. He studied Griffith. "Have you had any experience as an actor?"

"A little bit," said the writer.

"I'm looking for a man to play the lead in a story laid in Switzerland. It's a mountaineer-type part. We're going to call it *Rescued from an Eagle's Nest*. A baby is stolen from the yard where it is lying in the sun, and is carried off by a vicious eagle. The eagle is really a stuffed turkey we got at a taxidermist's. It's worked by invisible wires."

"It sounds promising," said Griffith.

"The hero climbs the mountain to the nest and has a terrific fight on a crag with the eagle."

"It sounds exciting," said Griffith.

"We're going to make some of it here in the studio, and some on the Palisades in New Jersey. That is where the fight with the savage eagle takes place. The man we had walked out on us this morning." He studied Griffith closely. "If you want to come tomorrow, you can play the part. There will be two days' work in it."

"I'll come, Mr. Porter," said David with as much enthusiasm as he could command.

"You go to the wardrobe section, look through the suits, and pick out something suitable to a mountain climber."

Griffith said he would pick out something suitable to a mountain climber and, after a few moments, left.

When he got home he was low in spirits. He slumped down in a chair, sitting far forward in it, with his long, lean legs stretched out in front, the way he so often sat.

"Did you sell your story?" Linda asked hopefully.

"Your husband is now leading man to a stuffed eagle," he said bitterly.

"You mean you got a job acting?"

"Yes. The big character-revealing scene is where I have a fearful struggle with the eagle on a crag in the mountains of Switzerland. It's nip and tuck for a while, then finally I get the eagle by the neck and choke the living daylights out of him. It'll bring people to their feet, cheering."

Linda was laughing. "It might lead to something," she said when she quieted down.

"I don't want it to lead to anything," said the bitter man. "I'm a writer, not an eagle fighter. I'm going to sell stories to the picture people. That'll keep us going. Meantime, I'll sell another play. You'll see!" His great, his almost overwhelming confidence in himself returned. "I'm meant for big things, Linda. I know that."

The next day he went to the studio, got his mountain-climbing suit, and fought a hand-to-hand struggle with the vicious eagle. The second day he got the baby out of the nest and carried it to its rejoicing parents.

"I want to see it when it's finished," said Linda.

"I don't. And I don't want anybody to know I was mixed

up in it. To admit you're acting in films is to admit you're a failure on the stage. Don't tell any of your friends, Linda. You won't, will you?" he appealed earnestly.

She promised.

He liked to work late at night, and after Linda had gone to bed in their miserable little flat he wrote with a lead pencil, erasing, rewriting. When he finished, he would put the pages away, so she would not see the manuscript, almost as if it were something sacred. And it was—to him. Stories went out, they came back, and each time one came back, it was a little stab in his heart. Most writers would have become discouraged, but not D. W. Griffith. His confidence in himself was supreme. He would win. Nothing—nothing in the world—could stop him.

The ebullient, self-confident Max Davidson came back. "Edison isn't the only studio," said the success-exuding Max of the "loud" clothes and Broadway manners. "There are four right now. Go and see good ol' Biograph. I told you about it before. Lots of real actors go there. They're glad to get that five. You go, too, Linda. You both might land."

"I'll go. I certainly will," she said.

"I've got a story in mind," said David. "Maybe I'll take it to them. Who's the man to see?"

"Wallace McCutcheon. He's as cold as a fish in January, but he pays out da mon'," said the lively Max.

The American Biograph and Mutoscope Company was housed in what had once been the very seat of aristocracy—a brownstone mansion with a fine curved iron railing leading up the steps from the street. Many social leaders and famous people had gone up those graceful steps—one was Stanford White. And now today, at this very moment, a tall, thin, confident man, with a way of thrusting his shoulders forward as he walked, mounted those steps. In an instant he was in a disordered world. There was the sound of pounding and sawing and of people shouting at each other and no one, seemingly, paying the slightest attention to anyone else. People in strange costumes rushed by, threading in and out among each other—so eager were they to get no place; at least it seemed that way. Some of the people had white smeared on their faces. Some of the men had on beards that wouldn't deceive a baby. Strange bluish vapor lamps blazed overhead, giving everybody a sickly, ghastly color. An old woman was sitting on a packing crate with a misshapen hat on her head and over her shoulders was a tattered shawl. When David passed in front of her, he saw that she was a girl made up to look like an old hag. The shoddy pretense sickened the sensitive man who had acted with Nance O'Neil. How unspeakably crude everything was! How cheap! How preposterous!

"Can you tell me where I can find Wallace McCutcheon?"

"In his office. He's making out the blue slips."

He found Mr. McCutcheon working at a disordered desk. He was a short man whose face had the appearance of having too many teeth. "What do you want?" Mr. McCutcheon was not a man to beat about the bush.

"Mr. McCutcheon, I'm the playwright David Wark Griffith. Maybe you've heard of my Play *A Fool and a Girl*."

Mr. McCutcheon said he hadn't had the pleasure.

"Mr. Hackett produced it." How much more impressive it sounded to say "Mr. Hackett" than to say "James K. Hackett." This showed one was of the theater. "It played in Washington." Without quite saying so, David gave the impression that the play had swept Washington off its feet. "I also write for *Leslie's Weekly*."

Mr. McCutcheon filed a blue slip. "What is it you have in mind?"

"Mr. McCutcheon," said the earnest man, "I've written a story called *Old Isaacs, the Pawnbroker*."

Mr. McCutcheon took the news calmly.

"Do you want me to tell it to you?"

Mr. McCutcheon filed another blue slip. "No."

"Do you want me to leave it?"

Mr. McCutcheon pondered this. "Yes," he said finally. "Yes, leave it," he said, and it was as if he had added " 'leave' is the key word." "Come back tomorrow and I'll let you know."

David Griffith walked back through the jumbled, mixed-up, crazy studio. The ragged old woman was eating out of a shoe box and licking her fingers.

When he got back to the grubby little apartment, Linda had a board on the table and was ironing. He told her the exciting news.

She was delighted. "Maybe I can get a job acting."

"You wouldn't want to act in what Fourteenth Street calls 'the fil-lums,' would you? If managers found it out you'd be on the banned list. Don't do it, Linda."

"I think it'd be fun."

"It wouldn't be my idea of contagious amusement," he said in the lofty manner he sometimes adopted.

As they had dinner, the two talked of the new world opening before them. If Mr. McCutcheon liked the story, he would write others, David said. Linda spoke again of going to the studio, and again he urged her not to do so.

When David returned, Mr. McCutcheon was again in his cramped office. Taking up the manuscript, he scrutinized it, as if he hadn't quite made up his mind. David tried to display an expression of complete confidence.

"I can use it," said Mr. McCutcheon at last. "We pay fifteen dollars."

"I'll take it, Mr. McCutcheon," said David with no pretense he was accepting a low price.

Shortly the picture was in production, so speedily were films made. David watched, fascinated. Ideas began to evolve in his head. What a vast difference there was between acting on the stage and in moving pictures. Most of the film people overacted, he felt.

Linda went to the studio and got a job. "I think it's a shocking comedown for you," David said. "If the uptown managers find it out, you'll never get a Broadway part."

"I've never had one, the way it is," she said.

He patted her shoulder in a fine moment of sympathy. "That's true, Linda. But you will! You're good-looking— you're really beautiful—and you've got talent. Your day will come."

"Maybe it'll come in moving pictures."

"I hope not, Linda. I certainly do. They're childish and I have no respect for them."

At night he worked in a kind of desperation on his manuscripts—this tall, thin, heavy-voiced man with his hooked beak of a nose, leaning over his writing table. On going to bed, he put the manuscripts in a box. There was an understanding between the two that Linda was not to fish around in the box. The box was sacred; it was not to be pried into, this little receptacle of dreams.

Also, after the way things were done, *Old Isaacs, the Pawnbroker,* was soon in the theaters. It was released March 26, 1908, and was nine hundred feet long. David did not go to see it. Another was *'Ostler Joe*, the retelling of a famous poem; it was released June 9, this same year. He did not bother to see it. Linda thought it was splendid.

Luck continued to walk with him. David sold other stories and, now that Mr. McCutcheon's attention had been directed to him, David was given acting parts, which he accepted, not with the elation that Linda experienced, but as a lowly way to make money.

Most of the actors, as soon as they got their hands on the money, slid out of the studio as fast as they could. Griffith stayed, watching the director, absorbed in the details of putting a scene on the screen. Mr. McCutcheon noticed this. One day he said, "Griffith, you seem to take an interest in things. How would you like to direct a picture?"

Griffith was taken by surprise. He didn't know whether he wanted to or not, he said. If he failed as a director, the studio would drop him and he wouldn't get another acting job.

"I promise you that if you fail I'll still keep you on as an actor," McCutcheon said.

"I'll take it, Mr. McCutcheon."

That night he told Linda the news. "Now you'll get some place," she said.

"It'll give us some money until I sell something," he said.

Griffith began to turn over in his mind how he would direct a picture, and the details he would give it.

The title that had been clapped on the story was *The Adventures of Dolly*. Dolly was a baby who got mixed up in as strange an adventure as anybody could want. She was kidnaped by gypsies; when pursuers were hard upon their trail, they put the unlucky child in a barrel and sent her down the river and over the falls. It would make people hold their breath, said the now friendly Mr. McCutcheon. The story was silly but it was a chance to direct. David certainly wasn't going to direct a flicker the way they did a stage play. He'd watched other directors long enough to have that firmly in his mind. What if he did fail? He could sell other stories and probably a play. He would direct the picture as he wished, let the wintry winds of the front office roar. He didn't have to make a living this way.

He tore into the picture and he tore into it in his own way. Instead of placing the camera in front of the scene, as if this were a stage, he picked up the camera and moved it around. McCutcheon was shocked; he'd made a mistake in his man; besides this man was spending money like a sailor at Coney Island. It was too late to change directors; maybe they could get some of their money back.

Down the river in the bobbing, whirling barrel went poor Dolly—the barrel operated by hidden wires. The most breath-taking scene was when the barrel went over the falls. The grief-stricken parents frantically opened the barrel—and there was Dolly, smiling a big, happy, heart-warming smile, not a scratch on the innocent little thing.

The picture opened at Keith & Proctor's Union Square Theatre, July 14, 1908. In the theater David's ear had been attuned to audiences; now he used this ability again. If the audience wanted this kind of picture, let 'em have it.

The exciting year of 1908 continued. David sold other stories; he directed other pictures. Other directors were in awe of their pictures. But D. W. wasn't. He said, "In a legitimate theater the audience listens to the actors; in a motion-picture theater, they watch them."

During this time Linda had been getting jobs and now, as his power and authority increased, he said, "I'll give you jobs, but don't let anyone know we're married."

The secret marriage continued. He called her "Miss Arvidson."

The business office looked on him with a cold and appraising eye. He was not making pictures the way they'd been made since they started. He was yanking the camera around as if it were a puffball.

The belief was that when an actor walked, his feet had to show, or the audience would say he was walking on air and not take the picture seriously.

One day the shocked Mr. McCutcheon came to David in great distress. "I've just been looking at your new picture, Griffith, and you've cut the people's feet off. They're walking on air."

"The audience won't notice that."

"They will, and they'll titter."

"There won't be a titter in the house," said David. "I know what I'm doing."

"I do, too. You're ruining us. The theaters will refuse to book our pictures. The Trust is after us hot and heavy, as it is."

Mr. McCutcheon was thoroughly and completely alarmed by the actions of the new director he'd taken on.

Griffith had one fact fighting on his side. Biograph was sickly; some thought it might not pull through the winter. It was selling fifteen prints of an average picture. *Dolly* jumped the number to twenty, which made the business office blink. Calls were coming in for "AB" pictures made by that new director, for his name was not known even to the trade. It had never been on the screen and it had never been in a trade magazine. If, for some astounding reason, the business office had wanted him to put his name on a picture, he would have used Lawrence Griffith. His stories and plays were going out under his full name.

Mr. McCutcheon spoke to him again about cutting people's feet off. Griffith, feeling sure of himself, said he was going to continue cutting 'em off. Mr. McCutcheon left, pretty well shaken.

Linda made David take her to the halls where these new moving pictures were shown. He looked down on them. Why should he—an intellectual—a man who loved the classics—a man who read and reread *Leaves of Grass*—a man who had great thoughts about the meaning of life and man's place on this insecure little blob called "the earth"—why should he have to fashion pictures for monkey-minded people? It was bitter. He would make some more money and then throw the whole sickening thing over. Then he would become a playwright to be reckoned with—maybe a Sardou, or a Sudermann.

Linda liked pictures. She began going with her friends, leaving David at home. He welcomed this; it gave him a chance to write. From time to time he got out *The Treadmill* and studied it. If he could get it just right, it would be a great, a moving stage play—a play of significance—not an absurd and ridiculous thing like an eagle carrying off a baby by the diapers.

Striking as his personality was, and great as his thoughts might have been, there was one trait he had hardly at all. The completely honest, the earnest, the sincere, the incredibly ambitious man had little or no sense of humor. The small bit he had was of a burlesque nature. Sometimes he would imitate a Negro preacher. At bottom he liked Negroes and, he said, understood them. Sometimes he spoke with affection of the mammy he'd had as a child. He spoke of his mother, who was living in Louisville and to whom he was now sending money. Most of all he spoke of his father—a great, a forceful, a Shakespeare-loving aristocrat who had given up his life, through his war wounds, to protect a section of the country that carpet-baggers had come into, carpetbaggers who had aroused the Negroes against their old and sympathetic masters.

Meantime, his importance was increasing. He was the "money" director. He spent more money than the other directors, but, on the other hand, he made more.

As he brought the camera closer and closer, he saw that the face projected on the screen showed every line and wrinkle—far, far more than could be seen on the spoken stage. So he began selecting the boys and girls who came to the studio on whose faces there were no lines. The other directors were taking "experienced" actors from the spoken stage.

He was not a hail fellow well met; instead, he was distant and aloof. Everybody at the studio was called by the first name, but no one called him "Dave." He was "Mr. Griffith," or "D. W." Sometimes he was called "The Boss." He liked this.

One day Mr. McCutcheon brought up a man and said, "Billy's going to be your photographer from now on."

Billy Bitzer was shorter than Griffith, with powerful shoulders and thick, stubby fingers. His full name was Gottlieb Wilhelm Bitzer. He was born in Boston, of a German family, and had a slight German accent. He was a genius in handling machines. The camera was a heavy, complicated affair that no one understood very well. If anybody knew its whims, that gifted person was Billy Bitzer, who lived only to experiment with his fascinating toy. After the studio closed at night, he would stay and work with his camera and film, mixing solutions and making tests. The thing he was proudest of in all the world was that he had made the first news pictures in America—William McKinley on the lawn of his home being notified of his nomination for President. He loved to have the actors, and the strange characters that inhabited the half-mad studio, ask him about the Great Event.

"Yess, I take de picture," he would say. "It help elect heem President. Pictures were shown in Mutoscope boxes in Mr. Hammerstein's Olympia Theatre, in New York, October 12, 1896. Effrybody could hardly believe their eyes."

Billy was the studio's most powerful production man. He had joined Biograph in 1896 as an electrician, but was soon "fussing" with cameras. He had become head cameraman; lesser people feared him as they would the plague. He was the one who determined if the lights were strong enough, if the angles were right, and who instructed the actors how rapidly they could gesture; in fact, he was the boss of the picture and was, indeed, the best cameraman in America.

Billy had seen Griffith as an actor—and he didn't think much of him. Billy had charge of all camera work in the studio, and now an actor, who thought he could direct, had been thrown on his back.

"Dis is de way I do," said Billy to the greenhorn. "I have read de story and I am ready to explain what you must do."

He showed Griffith a laundry shirt cardboard which he had divided off into columns by drawing lines with a lead pencil.

"Here is de picture de way we make it," he announced.

He pointed to the columns

COMEDY   DRAMA   SADNESS   PRETTY SCENE

"Now I have study de picture. Comedy is what we need more of."

With his lead pencil he made two X's under Comedy so that it read:

COMEDY
  XX

"We need more for de pretty scene, like dis"—

PRETTY SCENE
  XXX

"Now for sadness zo"—

SADNESS
  X

"See. Dere is de picture for you, like I do it for effrybody."
He proudly thrust the cardboard into Griffith's hand.

Griffith studied the cardboard and he studied Billy who was
so proud of his work—Billy who knew so many things he
himself didn't.

"I think I understand, Billy. But I am the one who directs
the picture. I tell you what to do."

Billy looked at him in shocked amazement. "It is always
done zo, Mr. Greeffith."

"Not when I direct, Billy. I do it my own way."

"You don't vant no cartbort?"

"No. I have studied the story and I have everything in my
head."

It was a moment before Billy could speak. "You mean—no
cartbort?"

"No. No cardboard."

"Yoost your headt?"

"Yes. Just my head."

"It is badt."

After a little more discussion, the poor fellow went to an-other part of the studio, convinced he would never get along with this crazy new director that had been thrust on him.

Griffith threw himself into the making of motion pictures with incredible energy. It was as if some private demon haunted him and he wanted to prove something to it. When he started across the studio, he did not walk so much as run. He infused others with his driving desire to get things done; the whole studio was electrified. But also mystified. He wasn't directing pictures the way other people directed them. He was doing things that were downright crazy. But his code num-bers were coming up faster than any other director's. What was it this aloof, impersonal, driving man had?—this man who was always having trouble with the business office?—this man who seemed to have no respect at all for the men gripping the moneybags.

Linda was delighted that he gave less time to the matter of writing which was going to get him nowhere. Seven hundred dollars for a play! Six dollars for a poem! He gave her work in pictures. One or two of the regular workers began to suspect they were married, but it was well to be circumspect. And so matters rested.

August 17, 1908, came—a big day, indeed, for on that day he signed a contract with Biograph, as it was called, for fifty dollars a week. But he did not sign his real name; he signed it "Lawrence Griffith." No one in the theater world must know that the author and playwright was having anything to do with the shoddy kind of entertainment called moving pictures.

That evening, when he got home, he took out his Indian clubs, stripped down, and began to swing them. "Linda," he said, as he swung them, "I've got something to tell you. Good news, ma'am."

"I wish you wouldn't always swing those clubs when you have something important to tell me. Do one thing at a time."

"It saves time, Linda. I try to get everything done that I possibly can."

"What's the good news? Did you sell another fifteen-dollar story?"

"It's bigger than that, Linda. I signed a contract with the studio today."

"For how much? You know what a poor businessman you are."

"I did pretty well this time. I'm to get fifty dollars a week, plus a commission, until it mounts up to another fifty."

"They'll probably try to beat you out of your commission."

"I don't think so, Linda. They're fair-dealing people."

She was delighted with his news and the two talked together for some moments, then, looking at him closely, she said, "David, you seem depressed."

"No, I'm not," he assured her. "I'm just tired. I want to take a nap." He put the Indian clubs away.

One of the things he could do was to sleep in a chair.

Thrusting his long legs out in front of him and resting his chin on his hand, he closed his eyes and was soon asleep. Linda moved quietly about the little apartment, preparing dinner.

One of Griffith's problems was the kiss. If it were held too long, rude boys in the audience made catcalls and ugly noises. The women, however, liked to see the kiss delivered as if it meant something.

"Billy, can't you do something about the kiss?"

"Maybe zo," said Billy.

After experimenting, Billy attached a large iris diaphragm on the front of his camera; to this diaphragm device was a handle that served as a weight. When time came for the troublemaking kiss, Billy cranked with one hand; with the other he released the iris handle and slowly the weight closed the opening and slowly the scene faded out in a love-drenched mood. This solved the kiss problem. No catcalls.

CHAPTER 3

HIS SECRET MARRIAGE
CONTINUES

THERE TURNED UP AT THE STUDIO A HULK OF young man standing over six feet and weighing more than two hundred pounds. This was his birthday—January 17, 1909 —and he was twenty-nine years old. He had extraordinarily large feet and hands and a kind of slow-witted look. He said that he was a comedian. To prove it, he carried a calling card that said MACK SENNETT, ACTOR AND COMEDIAN.

This strange, unplaced young man had been born on a farm in Canada where his family had lived for more than a hundred years. He was Irish-Canadian, could speak Canuck French, and something that sounded very much like English. His family gave up the farm and landed in the United States; the boy got a job in a steel mill where he helped to carry beams and huge weights; he was just the person for this. He was slow, slap-footed, and dependable.

After a time the family moved to Northampton, Massachusetts, where he took another whack at school. At about this time he began to fancy himself as a singer; it seems he was alone in this. Also he began to think of himself as an actor. This was something that must be faced. He began to talk about New York and going on the stage. No one would seem less equipped for such a career than this young former steel-mill worker who moved his lips on the occasions when he undertook to read.

He had prudently saved his mill money and, finally, left for New York, ready to bring Broadway to its knees. Broadway, knowing nothing of this, went along as usual. It was the old story of doors that did not open. Finally he was offered a job in the Bowery Theatre. The tempting offer was to be the hind legs of a horse. This was somewhat less than he had dreamed back in the mill, but hind legs were better than no legs at all. Another man was the front legs. The situation was a happy one for Mack, for it turned out that the hind legs were much more important than the front ones, for the hind legs were the ones that kicked and indulged in funny antics. The young man liked this and thought up strange and unexpected kicks that delighted the fun-loving audience. Another performer on the stage was "Little Egypt," a local girl with special talents.

Mack had advanced his act about as far as he could, so he asked if he could go out on the stage and sing a funny song. The manager, sobered by the request, told him to try his luck. Music was arranged, and the young man walked out on the stage alone and faced an audience who had not the slightest idea that they had once been vastly amused by the singer's comic gifts.

The music struck up. He sang.

When the matter was over, the manager said he thought, everything considered, that the young man had better go back to his first love.

His love, however, had cooled, and he started to look for another job.

"Why don't you try fil-lums?" one of his friends asked.

"Where should I go?"

"The Biograph studio is on East Fourteenth Street. Lots of people who are at liberty go there."

"Who do I ask for?"

"D. W. Griffith is the director and does the hiring."

In no time at all the at-liberty actor was walking up the winding steps of the old brownstone mansion.

"I want to see Mr. Griffith. Where can I find him?"

"He's all over the place. He'll be wearing a floppy hat."

After a time he found Griffith—Griffith tall and thin and intellectual; Sennett tall and heavy and ponderous who cared for reading hardly at all.

"I'm an actor," said Sennett. "I'd like to work for you."

The cold, impersonal, aloof man inspected him in detail. "What kind of actor?"

"I'm a comedian."

The director's face went down. "I'm not making comedies."

"I also dance and sing," said the young stalwart.

"I'm sure you do them well, but at present I have no opening for your obvious talents."

The young singer lumbered off but did not leave the studio; there were other directors, and finally he landed a job. The young fellow might not look like an intellectual, but his brain was active and he was observant. Instead of dashing out of the studio the moment he was free, as most actors did, he remained, watching the directors at work. Griffith appealed to him most of all. Indeed Griffith was the rising director, the one talked about, the one spoken of with respect, even if he was no back-slapper.

Griffith was hard to cultivate. A hundred actors were upon him; sometimes they waited at the foot of the stone steps and pounced on him, but he shook them off. He was always busy, always in a rush; he was inordinately ambitious; he would direct pictures the way he thought best, let the front office roar. But now, as the financial men examined the money sheets, they roared less and less. Sometimes they almost praised him. The situation was incredible.

Sennett hung around Griffith like a bear around a bee tree. One of the problems was the tremendously heavy camera and now, under Griffith's direction, it often had to be moved. When the moment came, Sennett plucked up the monster as if it were a toy on a what-not shelf and took it where Griffith designated. This suited little Billy Bitzer—it was goot to have somebody do eet. But even this kindly act did not get good Mack Sennett anywhere.

At other times he stood handily out of the way and watched Griffith direct. This was Heaven.

He discovered that after work hours Griffith walked alone to his flat. Sennett waited for him, pretending that it was just an accident the two should meet, and paced along with him. Here, Sennett found, Griffith was more approachable than at other times. He asked Griffith about his theory of directing, a subject that, just now, was of absorbing, almost overwhelming interest to Griffith. His theory, in short, was that nothing should be done as it was on the stage. No full-arm gestures. A favorite phrase of his was "Punctuate with the camera." This seemed to mean that the camera must break up long sequences. Once he said, "You've seen a Japanese foot juggler come out on the stage, lie down, place a mat under his head, and juggle a barrel with his feet. The audience is interested as long as the painted barrel keeps turning; the moment it stops, the audience loses interest. The director is the Japanese juggler; the story is his painted barrel—he must keep it turning." On another occasion he said, "I have an almost religious respect for the storyteller."

Sennett got a job under another director in *The Curtain Pole*.

This is a description of the story as given in an advertisement in a trade paper:

> *The Curtain Pole*. Length 765 feet. Code word: *Revibrestis*. Released Feb. 15, 1909.
> The plot: At the Edwards home there is a house party. Unfortunately Mr. Edwards has an attack of gout, which incapacitates him so as to throw the burden of arrangements on the women folks. When the guests begin to arrive, everything is in readiness, except the hanging of a pair of portieres. One of the guests is Mr. Du Pont, an ingratiating Frenchman, who wishes to help hang the curtains. He gets on a chair; the chair slips and he falls, breaking the pole. He insists upon procuring a new pole. Mr. Edwards tries to persuade him not to, but he says "Oui! Oui! I bring you ze one grand pole." Away he goes. He is but a short distance away when he meets a friend who invites him to sip a couple of absinthe frappes, after which he is more intensely charged with the phlogistic determination to get the pole. Arriving at the store, a pole is selected. He does not remember the width of the door, so he takes the whole length of the pole, 18 feet. Back he starts. *Gee whiz!* the limit. The absinthe frappe vapors, rising to his brain, make him a bit wobbly, and the pole in his hand becomes an instrument of destruction. After a series of indescribable incidents, he enlists the services of a cab, the driver of which is extremely boozy. Away goes this Pegasus, driven by a crapulous Eros, with a wild, vertiginous Frenchman as fare who holds the devastating pole across his lap, with 8 feet protruding on each side, mowing down everything within its reach—lampposts, fruit stands, market stalls, etc. All fall until at last the home of the Edwards is reached. Here, in the meantime, a pole has been gotten. He is a wreck as he enters with the pole; no one pays the slightest attention to him, which makes him furious. "Sacré bleu! Zis is ze ingratitude!" he says, and then in a rage, bites the pole in two.

As one reads this, he wonders about the strange writing in this outline meant for hurried film exhibitors. Here are three words you'll not meet with every day: phlogistic, crapulous, vertiginous.

Sennett, however, was proud of the picture and asked Griffith if he would look at it with him and give him points.

During the showing Griffith sat there, saying not a word, making not a movement. The two filed out of the little projection room.

"What do you think of it, Mr. Griffith?" asked the young comedian.

"Very funny," said Griffith. "I haven't laughed so much in years."

Sennett was hurt, but, on the other hand, Griffith had given up his time.

Sennett spoke of something near his heart. "Mr. Griffith, I would like to be a director myself and make a picture with funny policemen in it."

Griffith was aghast.

"Policemen are not funny," he said severely. "They represent law and order and should be respected as a part of our system of government."

"I was in a show once and I played a policeman an' the audience laughed."

"There must have been other elements. When I have a police officer in one of my pictures, I make him dignified and a person the audience can sympathize with. The important thing," continued Griffith, "is to tell a story."

"What about makin' them laugh?"

"In the whole length of a film an audience may laugh only a few times, but it will follow the story all the time."

The subject was dropped; the conversation went to something else.

Griffith's conflicts with the business office grew more frequent; he was not making the right kind of pictures, they said. Their biggest shock was when he said he wanted to make *Pippa Passes* by Robert Browning. No, they said; he wasn't going to put no poem on the screen with their money. But Griffith was strong and self-willed.

He was working only for money; with this he could get away from the debasing studio drudgery and do something fine. He scorned himself for not quitting, but there was the money that he and Linda must have to live. He paid no attention to the way in which other directors made pictures; he plunged fearlessly ahead, doing things that no one else had ever attempted. To do something new and different he accepted as a challenge and threw himself into this as if it were some kind of desperate adventure. Each new experiment was more radical and more expensive than the one before. What if it did fail? He did not care. He would soon be free from this monster. He would have a play on Broadway; the play would sway and move people and make them think. As its author he would be treated with respect; he would mingle with the great of the earth. This strange, almost incredible man continued to dream and to work. His driving energy was prodigious. He never seemed to be tired, except in the morning when it was time to go to the studio.

His secret marriage to Linda continued; no one knew of their union. In 1908 he put her in a picture called *Lines of White on a Sullen Sea.*

A happy evening for him was to go to a stage play with Linda; on the way home the two would discuss the plot of the play. She was more interested in the acting and preferred to talk about that. Sometimes she spoke slightingly of his writing. Directing was the big thing, she said. She had a group of friends and often went to a picture show with them. When he was alone he got out his manuscripts, humping his bony shoulders over the table, and writing with a lead pencil. When he heard her returning, he put his writing away.

She still cooked his meals. Sometimes, when he was late, he telephoned her and stopped at a restaurant, so as not to delay her in her household duties.

One morning he went to the window and looked into the bleak back yard and said, "I want you to telephone the studio I'm sick and can't come today."

"You'd better not do that, David," she said. "You're getting ahead so wonderfully as a director. You'll make your mark."

"In water," he said bitterly. "Directing a film is writing in water. Poetry lives."

"Directing lets us live," she said.

Billy Bitzer had thought of himself as the genius of the studio—and he was almost that, indeed. No one had ever had such command of the camera as he had. He liked to stay at night after the others had gone and "fool around mit the camera." When he had been assigned to Griffith, he had regarded Griffith with great suspicion. He had learned a great deal in working with other directors, and was prone to tell them how to manage a scene. But this new director had ideas of his own. Very explicitly he told what must be done. By mutterings and shakings of his head Billy said the matter could not be accomplished. One day Griffith said, "I want you to move the camera up close and fill the screen with just her head."

Billy stared in utter unbelief. "You mean you vant a head mit no body upon der screen?"

"Yes."

"It is not done dot way."

"It's done that way here."

Billy went ahead with his work, certain he had been as-signed to a director who would soon be on the street.

When the picture was run off in the little cubbyhole of a projection room, Mr. McCutcheon and the money men thought they were in the hands of an experimentalist who would soon ruin them.

When the trying evening was over and Griffith was home, he told Linda what had happened.

"I think you'd better do what they want."

"Let them fire me if they want to. I think I've got a stage play that's just right."

"I think you're making a mistake."

"Have faith in me, Linda. You'll see. Someday you'll be proud of me."

"I'm proud of you now," she said sincerely.

A strange procession of characters came to that brownstone former mansion: out-of-work actors, jugglers, contortionists, men taking bets on horse races, villainous moneylenders, mothers with darling children; and, sometimes, exceedingly attractive girls. Some of the latter had tried for chorus jobs in the big Broadway shows but had failed; then word had got to them of the gold mine on Fourteenth Street. Here they came —this weird, impossible segment of the world of entertainment.

One who came was a girl of fifteen. Her father had died in a strange, almost unbelievable accident which could happen only once in a hundred years. John Charles Smith was purser on a side-wheeler running between Toronto and Lewiston, on Lake Erie. The night the boat landed in Toronto he was in a hurry to see his family, rushed out of the cabin, hurried down the passageway, and started to jump over the drive shaft that turned the great wheels. An iron pulley was hanging down, his head struck the pulley, and he fell to the deck. He was soon dead, leaving a widow twenty-four years old and three children—the eldest five; she was Gladys Mary Smith. The mother—a determined, strong-willed woman—decided to take her three children to New York and give them a start in the world. Her success was quite startling. There was a Chauncey Olcott play on Broadway entitled *Edmund Burke*. In this were the three Smith children: Mary, Charlotte, and Edith. They danced and sang remarkably well, especially little Edith.

Mary had accomplished something quite astonishing, even for volatile, quick-changing Broadway; at the age of fifteen she had got a job with the great, the one-and-only, the almost-holy David Belasco in *The Warrens of Virginia*.

Belasco thought they could get a name more original than Smith and asked Mary about the names in her family. Mary, as they discussed the matter, said that back in Ireland her grandmother's name was Elizabeth Denny Pickford.

"Pickford," repeated Belasco. "That's it! You are Mary Pickford."

And now little Edith Smith changed her name to Jack Pickford, for, all along, little Edith had been a boy.

The play went out on the road and was a success. After a time it ceased and Mary Pickford wanted something to tide her to her next play. Word of the gold mine got to her, and up the fateful brownstone steps she went.

There was no doorman, no one to ask why? She walked into what, after the chaste seclusion of a Belasco rehearsal hall, was a madhouse. People in grotesque costumes and startling make-up dashed here and there, seemingly not quite certain where they were going but in a tremendous rush to get there.

"Mr. D. W." was an actor in films before he became a director. Here he is adorned with a wig. In early pictures many actors wore wigs to disguise themselves from their friends. *Culver Service.*

The boy: Ben Alexander; later he became famous in "Dragnet." And D. W. Griffith. *Culver Service.*

Griffith often posed Mary Pickford with rabbits in order to portray youthful innocence. *DeGaston.*

Douglas Fairbanks, Mary Pickford, Charlie Chaplin, and Griffith. Griffith was hard on his stars, but they loved and respected him. *Culver Service.*

D. W. Griffith as he looked on a set when directing a picture. *Culver Service.*

Mae Marsh as "the little sister" in *The Birth of a Nation*. *Culver Service*.

The Reverend Thomas E. Dixon from whose novel *The Birth of a Nation* was made. *Culver Service*.

Henry B. Walthall as "the Little Colonel" at the time he played the lead in the picture at $75 a week. *Culver Service.*

The immortal love-sick scene from *The Birth of a Nation*. This brought great laughter from audiences. Lillian Gish and an extra, later identified as Walter Freeman. *Culver Service.*

Linda Arvidson appearing in the motion picture *As the Candle Burns*. Griffith was secretly married to her. *Culver Service*.

Carol Dempster was a dancer in the Ruth St. Denis group. She became important in Griffith's life. The gentleman: W. C. Fields. *Culver Service*.

Griffith at his second wedding, which took place in Louisville, Kentucky. His widow lives in New York City. *Courier-Journal and Louisville Times.*

On the left: Griffith and his bride shortly after his second marriage. The people on the right are Louisville friends. *Courier-Journal and Louisville Times.*

Griffith was proud of his family. He had his father's military record carved on the tomb, which stands today near the village of Crestwood, Kentucky.

The house Griffith bought for his mother in LaGrange, Kentucky. Griffith came here to write and here dictated stories to his wife and a stenographer. The stories did not sell. On the front porch—the author of this book.

Men in impossible beards hurried by. Children clung to their mothers' hands. Carpenters pounded; men shouted; no one seemed to know what they shouted, or to care. People were eating—they always seemed to be eating in this strange mental infirmary. A man with a monkey sitting on his shoulder threaded his way through the crowd. The monkey was the only one who seemed to be at home.

"I want to see Mr. Griffith," she said.

"He's over there," the man said.

She approached the man with the big hat. "Are you Mr. Griffith?"

The man gave her a chilling look. "Can't you see I'm busy?"

"I asked you a respectful question."

"It so happens I am," said the man less belligerently.

The two sized each other up. She did not think much of what she saw.

"I'm an actress and I'd like to get a job with you."

How many times he'd heard that! He'd settle her; he turned to look, then looked again. Here was an exceedingly attractive girl with long, beautiful golden curls and a winsome expression.

"Have you had any experience?"

"I have," said the girl, who was completely able to take care of herself. "I am a David Belasco actress."

"Do you mean you acted for him?"

"In *The Warrens of Virginia* by William C. De Mille."

He was impressed. Why, he himself, after all his years on the stage, had not been good enough to act for the great man. "What part did you play?"

"Betty Warren. Cecil B. De Mille played the part of my brother."

He came down in his manner.

"If you're good enough for Belasco, why do you want to come here?"

"Because I want the money."

"Do you know how much we pay?"

"I hear it's five dollars a day. But you'll have to pay me ten dollars."

"Nobody gets that much."

"I do," said the confident young lady.

An idea came to him. "I'm making *Pippa Passes* by Browning. I'll try you out here and now."

"What do I have to do?"

"You carry a guitar and pretend you're playing and singing. Let me see you do it."

A guitar was brought.

She strummed her way across the set.

"You're engaged. I'll put make-up on you."

He got the make-up box and dabbed some white on her face. In a few minutes the scene was made.

"Here's your blue slip. Go to the business office and you can get your money."

"How much do I get?"

"Five dollars."

"I told you what I get," said the firm-minded girl.

He made out a new slip and gave it to her, defeated by this assured beauty who had swum into his studio.

With two temperamental people working together sparks were sure to fly. One day Mary came to the studio and with her came Charlotte—and Lottie had quite a bit of temperament herself. The picture was *To Save Her Soul*. In it Mary was to play a wronged church-choir singer, a part just then very popular with a shocked but eager public.

The scene called for the stark drama that Griffith loved so

well. Mary had on a velvet dress with a long train; the dress was fastened in the back with safety pins and was none too sturdy. Under no circumstances was she to turn her back to the camera. The scene began. The man who had deceived Mary wanted her to come with him; when she refused, he whipped out a pistol and pointed it at her. Arthur Johnson, who was playing the part, had consumed too many beers at lunch and was now in such a hazy state that he could hardly hold his wobbly pistol. Mary tried to look frightened out of her wits, but was not able to "get into" the scene. Griffith rehearsed it several times, but still she didn't play it as he wished. Suddenly his temper flared and, seizing her roughly by the shoulders, he shook her, shouting, "What's the matter with you? Can't you play it with feeling?"

Mary was so shocked to have him shake her, so outraged, that she fought back, and the fragile dress fell apart. "How dare you lay hands on me?" she cried.

"To teach you how to act."

"I can act."

"You can't. You're a stick of wood."

She bit him.

Before the astonished man knew what was happening, Lottie rushed at him and began to pummel him with her fists, and to kick him, screaming at the top of her voice, "How dare you do that to my sister, you horrid man?"

He stared at the two outraged girls. "Get out of here, you wild cats!" he roared.

"We'll get out and we'll stay out!" said Mary and, picking up the train of her velvet dress, swept out of the set. When she got to the little cubbyhole that was her dressing room, Lottie began to take out the safety pins. When the dress was off, Mary threw it on the floor, got into her street clothes, and soon the two girls were on the street.

Griffith had had a few minutes to think and now hurried after the enraged girls. "Excuse me, Mary," he said contritely. "My nerves were on edge. I'm truly sorry. Come on back; let's finish the picture and be friends."

After a time Mary went back to her cubbyhole, rescued the dress, and soon was again on the movie set, facing the wobbly pistol. The bitter struggle had aroused her; the scene went off like a dream.

Griffith and Mary Pickford continued to work together, each gaining respect for the other. But Mary wanted money; she was adamant. Griffith, pressed by the business office, could not give it to her.

Pippa Passes was released October 4, 1909—the first motion picture the New York *Times* ever reviewed. The *Times* (October 10, 1909) said, "The motion picture audiences have received it with applause and are asking for more." Griffith had won out in his struggle with the business office—at least for the time being.

To Save Her Soul also was released. The scene where the despicable man threatened the innocent choir singer sent shivers down the backs of the audience. The pistol never once wobbled.

CHAPTER 4

HE MAKES A TWO-REEL PICTURE
—THE MANAGEMENT IS
SHOCKED

IT IS ALMOST INCREDIBLE HOW FAST GRIFFITH worked and how many one-reel pictures he made—and how good they were. However, he held them in contempt—he'd make them his way, let the whirlwind come. He said, "I have to earn a living in this sorry mess in order to so something worth-while."

He had grown up in the shadow of the War Between the States; his father had told him tales of the war years and "reconstruction," and now, fired by all this, he began to write a history of the Civil War. Busy as he was, he found time to read war books and to make notes. He would show the South's point of view.

And now he wrote more and more in secret. At first he had dictated parts of his play to Linda, but he no longer did so. His plays came back; when this happened there was a forced silence between the two. Once he had sung plantation songs for her amusement; now he ceased.

He was a constant puzzle to Billy Bitzer. "It ees not done zo, Mr. Greeffith," he would say.

"It is done zo mit us, Billy," he would say.

The first picture of his new star to be released was *The Violin Maker of Cremona;* it was released June 7, 1909, and was considered one of the best pictures Biograph had made. Another picture Mary Pickford played in was *The Lonely Villa*—written by none other than Mack Sennett who still was secretly yearning to make a picture about funny policemen. In the isolated house, as related by the former ironworker, was the mother and with her were her three little daughters. Bad men came and pounded on the door. One of the villainous men was Mack Sennett, disguised in a magnificent beard. At the last moment the mother and her three terrified daughters were rescued and all was well in the once-troubled villa. Mack Sennett did better financially than any other member of the cast, for he got fifteen dollars for the story and five dollars each for the two days he worked. Motion pictures were definitely progressing.

The exhibitors were beginning to ask, "What's happened at Biograph? It's the best in the business."

The studios stole stories right and left. If someone had suggested to a studio manager that an author should be paid, the studio manager would have looked at the man as if he were mad. In 1909 Biograph stole Jack London's *Just Meat*, a story of Alaska. The title was changed to *For Love of Gold* and the story given to Griffith.

The story dealt with two thieves who began to distrust each other. In the climax, the drama depended on what each thief was thinking. In other words, the audience should be able to read the minds of each. The method that had always been used was by what was called "dream balloons." This was a bit of double-exposure in which the "dream balloon" told what was going on in the person's mind.

Griffith had an idea. Instead of setting up the camera and photographing the scene from beginning to end without moving the camera, he would pick up the camera and bring it near enough the actors to show every expression on their faces. He told Billy what he wanted.

Billy looked at him incredulously. "You mean pick oop the camera, when de scene is going on, and carry it around? Excuse me, Mr. Greeffith, it is not done."

"We'll do it," said Griffith, and after a great deal of grumbling Billy picked "oop" the camera.

The story came alive. Audiences could see an actor's face and understand what he was thinking. No one knew it but this was a bill of divorcement between stage and cinema.

The business office did not like the innovation. The exhibitors would not like the change, the business office said. Their audiences expected a certain kind of picture and would not like crazy ideas.

Billy warned Griffith of the business-office attitude.

"I'm going to move the camera still closer in my next picture," said Griffith.

"It ees not done, Mr. Greeffith," said the beaten man.

Griffith was revolutionizing motion pictures—nothing less. He invented, or introduced, startling innovations: the close-up, the long shot, the moving camera, the vista, the vignette, the fade in, the fade out, the iris effect, the high-angle shot, the low-angle shot, back lighting, the so-called "Rembrandt lighting." On top of this he advanced the art of storytelling by cutting and editing. He discovered how to show two lines of action in different places at the same time and not addle the audience. In the realm of motion-picture making he was doing what was almost unbelievable.

At first, in the studio, among the employees, he had been "D. W."; then he had become "Mr. D. W." Now he was being referred to as "The Master." This praise and adulation meant nothing to him. He looked down on it—and went on working secretly at home on something that would be worth-while.

No player was known by name. This was exactly what Biograph wanted. If anybody knew the names of the players, they might ask for more money—a shocking situation. In spite of this, now and then a letter wandered in addressed "To the little girl with the long curls." In subcaption, in one of the pictures, Griffith referred to her as "Little Mary." Immediately she became known as "Little Mary."

No exhibitor in America knew the name of D. W. Griffith, which was as he wanted it. When he signed a contract, he was Lawrence Griffith; when he got anything published, he was David Wark Griffith. "Wark" was a family name on his mother's side.

Griffith worked in his own way, telling no one in the management what he was doing. And he worked from no outlines; the word "scenario" hadn't been invented. He did not even use notes. It was all in his head. When time came to rehearse a scene, he told the actors what was going to happen and how they should react and what kind of characters they were to interpret. No actor knew the beginning of a story nor how the story ended.

Jeremiah J. Kennedy, the chief owner of the company, came to Griffith on the set and asked him what he was doing. Griffith told him he was making *Enoch Arden,* the famous poem by Tennyson.

"Why, that's a poem!"

"But a good one."

"It has no action and no chase," persisted the shocked man.

"It has mental drama."

"Things that happen inside your head can't be shown."

"I can show them," said the confident young man.

"How long will it be?"

"Two reels," said Griffith.

The other was aghast. "The exhibitors will not book it. Cut it down to one reel of fourteen minutes."

"It takes two reels to tell the story."

"But we can't sell it."

The manager left, believing that Griffith had realized his mistake and was going to change the film. A few days later the manager was invited into the tiny projection room; he was shocked at what he saw.

"I thought I told you to put it in one reel."

"I'm sorry, but it couldn't be done," said Griffith.

The manager released one reel, May, 1911, with word that the second reel would be sent next week. There were, however, so many telephone calls and telegrams that the manager had to give in and let the exhibitors have the two reels together. It was a humiliating experience.

The business office kept pressing Griffith to turn out the pictures—get in the money. He was willing to turn out the pictures, but he wanted them to be artistic. The business office couldn't understand such a farfetched point of view. If a picture made money, it was artistic. The business office had a way of driving straight to the point.

Everybody dashed off stories. The actors wrote them while waiting at the studio. The stories were turned over to the editor who accepted some; as to the others, he followed the immemorial way of editors.

The story standard, however, was rising and, after a time, stories became more difficult to come by. In May, 1910, when Griffith was in California, he decided to make a film of *Ramona*, the famous Indian love story by Helen Hunt Jackson. He paid her a hundred dollars for the story. The business office was shocked. What would greedy writers demand next?

In San Diego, R. Beers Loos was running a motion-picture theater. He had a daughter named Anita who saw the pictures from behind; the screen was thin, so it was easy to see the picture from behind. By twisting her neck a little, she could read the reversed subtitles.

"I can write stories as good as that," said the little miss, and forthwith set about it. When she finished, she climbed the iron ladder into the projection room, got the name Biograph and the address from the tin box that contained the reels, signed the name "A. Loos" to the story, and sent *The New York Hat* on its way.

After a reasonable length of time back came a check for fifteen dollars—a fortune.

The story came to Griffith, and he put Mary Pickford in it.

At this time an "uptown actor" (who hadn't been doing too well) heard about the gold mine and journeyed down to Fourteenth Street to see if he could strike pay dirt—Lionel Barrymore. Griffith was greatly impressed by the name and offered him a part in the picture.

Barrymore said, "Can I wear a wig?"

All knew what that meant—so friends would not recognize him.

"No," said Griffith, who wanted reality in his pictures.

Barrymore grumbled but went ahead and played the part. The pay was nice.

The studio did not relax in its determined efforts to keep Little Mary anonymous. One day, however, two girls showed up at the studio and told a kind of casual doorman they wanted to see Gladys Smith.

The man had never heard of her. "What picture has she been in?"

"*Lena and the Geese*," said one of the girls.

"I don't remember anybody named Smith in that picture."

"She has long curls."

A smile of understanding spread across his face. "Oh! I know," said the delighted man. "That's Little Mary."

He dashed off and in a few minutes came back with Mary of the Curls.

What a reunion that was—Mary and the Gish sisters. Little Mary and Lillian had been "child actresses." In a way, Lillian's story paralleled Mary's. She was born in Springfield, Ohio, and was three years younger than Little Mary. Lillian was the daughter of James Gish, a traveling salesman who contributed little or nothing to the support of the family and, almost before she knew it, Lillian was on the stage in a play called *Her First False Step*. This unfortunate step had been taken by her mother. The unspeakable man now wanted to get rid of the mother, but she would not let him go. The man warned the mother that if she did not let him go, she would regret it. He was connected with a circus and the circus had live lions, and the lions were on the stage, lashing their tails and showing their cruel teeth. They were, of course, in a cage. At exactly the right moment the heartless man seized little Lillian and threw her into the lions' cage—Lillian sending up a shriek that startled the lions.

However, it was not quite so dangerous as the audience believed. The cage had been contrived with great cunning. There was a sliding partition between the shrieking Lillian and the ferocious animals. The partition was operated by wires which could not be seen, even from the front rows. At the right moment the hero dashed in, snatched up Lillian, and dashed out, slamming the cage door behind him. From behind the scene the invisible partition was deftly opened and in rushed the savage, snarling beasts. So tense, so exciting was the scene that women in the audience fainted; strong men shuddered. But Lillian always made it, leaving the frustrated lions snarling.

Dorothy had been a child actress, too, but had never been thrown to the lions. However, night after night she'd had narrow escapes from express trains running at fearful speed just offstage.

Mary started to show her two old friends over the studio. On the way she met Mr. D. W.

"They're friends of mine," she explained; "they're actresses."

He looked at them with interest. "Mary, when you finish, bring them to me."

When they came, he talked to the two visitors, meanwhile studying them. "Come with me. I want to show you our new studio."

The three—Griffith and the two sisters—went into a studio filled with stage sets and a thousand odds and ends. "Walk ahead of me," he said. He made a silent signal to an electrician and suddenly the studio was flooded with garish Cooper-Hewitt lights that made the girls look like walking dead. Lillian wanted to leave, but she could not quite tell him so. "Walk ahead of me," he said again.

The two girls started on, their strange-acting host following them.

Suddenly, directly behind them, a shot rang out. The two whirled and there stood Griffith with a smoking pistol in his hand.

"Walk ahead of me," he said, and now the girls, believing they were in the hands of a madman, walked ahead at a lively pace. Another shot rang out and, when they turned, there he stood again, the smoking pistol in his hand. "I think it's going to be all right."

What did the man mean?

The explanation was not long in coming. He said he was going to start a picture which was to be called *The Unseen Enemy*. The climax dealt with two girls alone in a house, when burglars entered and soon discovered the girls. The terrified girls managed to get to the telephone and started to call the police. There was a stovepipe hole in the wall, and through this the burglars began to shoot at the girls. But the brave girls kept on telephoning; finally the police arrived and all was well, as things were at this time in his pictures.

"I wanted to see how you would stand up under fire," he said. "Come back tomorrow."

When they got there he could not tell them apart, so much alike did the sisters look, so he tied a blue hair ribbon on Lillian and a red one on Dorothy. They posed in the burglar picture, standing up heroically under fire. And thus, so casually, did people, at this time, become screen pioneers.

Most directors hurried through rehearsals—anything was good enough; no exhibitor ever complained about the quality of the acting. But Griffith didn't hurry.

He rehearsed until the actors were exhausted. "We'll run through it again." How well they knew that loud, self-confident, demanding voice with a slight southern accent. Over and over the scenes the players went, Griffith, with his floppy hat, watching them like a lynx. Poor acting enraged him. "I don't see why you can't do it," he would say harshly. "You're supposed to be an actor, aren't you? Do it this way." Then he would go through the part, never taking off his hat. "Remember, thought can be photographed. Is the audience reading your mind, or is your mind blank to begin with?" He was cruel and sarcastic. If a girl under his storming broke into tears, he would say, "Get the shower over and get into the scene." Sometimes the cast hated him. But in some strange way they were devoted to him. They learned more from him than from any other director. He was the greatest director in the world.

Calls came in for the pictures he directed. The business office watched him apprehensively. He might demand more money —a deplorable situation.

In spite of the efforts of the money men to hide the names and personalities of the players, the public was beginning to want to know more about the actors they saw on the screen. One morning Mary Pickford happened to start up the brownstone steps at the same time as Griffith did.

"Mr. Griffith, last night I met an old friend and she told me she had sent a letter to me in care of this studio. I've never got it."

Griffith, who had to work under the ruling of the business office, said, "The cast is not allowed to receive mail in care of the studio."

"If there is mail here for me, I have a right to get it," said Little Mary with large determination.

"I told you the rules. The letter'll have to go back."

"I want you to go to the business office with me and tell them to let me have my letter."

The two went to the business office, glowering at each other.

There were twenty-two letters; they had come in, not addressed by name but by description—"the little girl with the curls" being the most popular.

Little Mary was a bit awed herself. "I never had that many in all the time I was with Belasco." And now thrifty, money-conscious Little Mary said, "If I get that many letters I ought to be paid more."

A cold chill went down his back; and one went down the backs of the studio owners when Griffith told them the alarming situation.

Griffith himself was coming into conflict with this stern reality of the business office. He was spending too much money, the business office said. He was not being allowed enough, he said.

At about this time he made *The Battle at Elderberry Gulch*. I wrote Mae Marsh in Hermosa Beach, California, and asked if she had any memories of the making of the picture. Her answer:

"One thing that stands out in my memory is this. In the picture were Lillian Gish, Lionel Barrymore, Harry Carey, myself, and others. We were undergoing an Indian attack. At one place in the story Lillian Gish was sitting on the steps in front of the cabin. Harry Carey was to point a pistol at her, and this the brave Harry Carey did. But Lillian wasn't as frightened as Mr. D. W. thought she should be, so he touched Billy Bitzer on the shoulder, which meant for him to start the camera, then crept up behind Lillian and shot off the pistol. The effect was fine—Lillian almost jumped out of her skin and we escaped from the treacherous Indians."

David and Linda began to drift apart. She spoke belittlingly of his writings. Directing was going to get him ahead; writing wasn't. What had he to show for the time he had worked at writing? One play—a failure. Half-a-dozen plays that had interested no producer. A poem in a weekly; two or three articles in small, out-of-the-way magazines. His revenge was no longer to put her in the plays he directed. Instead of going home in the evening to eat dinner, he ate in restaurants, sometimes moodily by himself, sometimes with people from the studio. When he got home, he would not tell her where he had been, or with whom he had been. She felt he was hiding a great deal. The breach widened. He never dreamed now of singing plantation songs.

She no longer wanted to go to the studio where he was looked up to and admired, and began to go to the other studios. She was a pretty woman, and had talent. She did not tell him where or in what roles she was going to appear, for she, too, was becoming secretive.

One evening, when he came home, she wasn't there. Out to a picture show with some of her friends, he thought. This was his opportunity to write, and he got out his manuscripts.

After a time he heard a key in the door and Linda came in. He spoke briefly and went on with his work. Little as was the communication between them these days he was sensitive enough now to feel a change in her manner. There was an air of triumph about her.

"Here's something I think'll interest you." She held up a slip of paper.

He was mystified. What was she leading up to? That was her way, he'd found—beginning with something that seemed to have nothing to do with them, then suddenly presenting it full force. "It's a railroad pass to California."

She waited as if to enjoy what must be a shock to him.

"When are you going?" he asked.

"Tomorrow. I'm going to be leading lady for Kinemacolor!"

He began to pull at his fingers, as he so often did when under a strain. "You'd better make sure what you're doing. I don't think they're a very stable company."

"I do! I had a long talk with the president and he told me of their wonderful plans."

"They all have wonderful plans. I'll send you money, Linda. You've never been a woman to waste money, the way some wives are. I'll do the best I can by you."

She went into another room and began to prepare for bed. He sat, recovering from the shock. How quickly it had come! How sharp it was. How wonderful life had seemed when they had married five years ago. And now this. He sat for some moments, listening to the sounds she made, then again began to write.

CHAPTER 5

HE LONGS TO BE AN AMERICAN IBSEN

THE NEXT MORNING HE SLIPPED QUIETLY OUT to a restaurant and got breakfast. That evening, when he came home from the studio, Linda was gone. Everything was neatly in place, for she was a careful housekeeper. As he looked at the things, so orderly and so much like her, he reproached himself. He had not been as good a husband as he should have been. "Why didn't I try harder?" he asked himself.

The studio had given him some stories to read, but he couldn't keep his mind on them. The next morning she was still on his mind. He was late arriving at the studio. Billy Bitzer was already there, his cap turned around backward, peering through the lens piece of the camera. How lucky he was to have him. The two of them would do great things together.

"Billy," he said, "we'll go to California and make the finest pictures ever made and we'll make a lot of money. Then you can retire and fool around with your camera and I'll settle down and write. But I won't write anything for you to smear on film. I'm going to write for the stage and people of intellect. You'd be surprised if somebody, in the years to come, said to you that you'd worked with the American Ibsen, wouldn't you?"

"No, I would not be too surprised."

Something else was on his mind. "Billy, I'm upset. So look on me as charitably as you can if I snap at you."

Billy looked at the long, lean, bony, expressive face. "What is eet you would snap for, Mr. Greeffith?"

He told him what had happened, the two hovering over the camera as they talked. Carpenters carrying boards pushed by; each man seemed to have a cloth loop on the leg of his trousers, with a tool dangling in the loop. Each man, in the bib of his overalls, seemed to have a broad, flat carpenter's pencil with thick lead.

"It ees badt," said Billy, much touched. "I hate always to see married peoples go their own way. Maybe she come back. Maybe you go after her undt bring her back."

"I don't think I would do that, Billy"

"You cannot always tell what we will do sometimes most."

With Linda gone, Griffith could not take care of the apartment, so he asked the wife of the janitor if she could find him a maid. In a few days she said she had a prospect, and a time was set for an interview. When he got home, the janitor's wife, who was waiting for him, brought in a large colored woman with thick lips, a broad square face, and a wide nose. Her name turned out to be Cora Hawkins, and she was from Virginia. She had come up No'th because of the urging of her sister, but things hadn't turned out too well. "I don't feel at home heah," she said. "My ma gets my cousin to write me, because my ma don't write too good. She wants me come home."

He was delighted. Here was somebody he understood, somebody he sympathized with. And she, recognizing he was a southerner, understood him.

"Won't you sit down, Cora?" he said.

"Thank you," she said respectfully, and seated herself.

"I was brought up by a colored nurse," he said. " 'Auntie,' we called her. We all loved her."

Cora beamed. "Yes, suh. I know what she must been like. My ma say the wah change them so they ain't so much like they used to be."

"The war changed everything," he said feelingly. "People don't know what the South went through. The part after the war was worst of all—Reconstruction days."

"That's what my ma say."

"It ruined us. My father died of war wounds. We had to sell our farm and move to town. It was bitter."

"I know it must been," she said sympathetically.

He asked a delicate question. "Did your family fight for the Yankees?"

"No, suh," said Cora feelingly. "We true southern fam'ly."

The two continued to discuss the War Between the States, while the janitor's wife listened to this world she knew nothing about.

"I want to wuk for you, Mr. Griffith," said honest, sincere Cora, "but I must tell you, after a time I have to leave."

"Why is that, Cora?" he asked in surprise.

She dropped her eyes with the modesty of an old-time darky. "I'm carryin' a little one."

How many times he had heard that phrase in the South. "Oh!"

He was pleased she was so honest with him and was delighted with her. And so Cora went to work. She took a kind of possession of him. He was "high-class folks"—the kind she liked to work for.

He soon found that she had an infectious laugh that showed her fine, white, flashing teeth. Why, the people of New York never seemed to laugh so heartily as they did down South. Certainly the northern workers were not so loyal as the colored people of the South. Cora would be loyal to him, he thought.

He found she took great pride in her cooking and was pleased to have him bring home a guest; indeed, it never seemed to make any difference to her how many he brought; some way or other she managed to take care of them. What a treasure Cora was! How cheerful she was! What a fine representative of her race!

He continued to live in two worlds: one was the studio, the other was his secret writing. The two never crossed. He told no one at the studio about his writing, except that he had sold a few story outlines to motion pictures. And he told no one in the publishing business that he was connected with films. In addition, he had two personalities: in the studio he was an arrogant, dominating man who made people do as he wished—he feared no one. But for some strange reason when he met an editor, he was meek and humble.

His stories continued to come back. He would again put the story into the mail—soon it would again be back. These were bitter moments. Then he received a letter from S. S. McClure, editor of *McClure's Magazine*, which said, "We've had a favorable reading of your short story 'Redemption' and would like to have you call for an interview." These were thrilling words.

He slipped away from the studio and went to the magazine and soon was in McClure's private office. McClure was a small, spare man, with a sickly-looking mustache, reddish hair, and had, as Griffith soon observed, a way of rubbing the knuckle of his finger against his nostril. The tall, lean, hawk-nosed Griffith sat down and the two studied each other, as men do when they have dealings. A few words of general conversation followed, then McClure fumbled through his desk and pulled out the precious manuscript. To it was attached a carbon of the letter he had written Griffith.

"Yes, yes," said McClure, brushing his nostrils with his knuckle. "Yes, indeed," he added thoughtfully. "We have been impressed by your story. It has the feel of the kind of story we like. Our magazine is built on a certain theory and we stick to it. This quality is, I believe, called 'the McClure touch.' " The great editor smiled pleasantly. "However, we have decided the story is not for us. You must know," he added hastily, "this is no reflection on the story. It's only our point of view." He smiled the cold, impersonal smile that has chilled the blood of a million writers. "I cannot point out details—that would take too long. Remember, I am speaking only from our point of view." He smiled another chilling smile. "If you write another story, I wish you would address it to me personally." He removed his eyes from Griffith and began to shuffle the papers on his desk, clearing his throat as he did so.

Griffith arose, humble and repressed, stuffed the manuscript into his pocket, thanked the great editor for his kindness, and left. It was not long until he was back in the studio, again the arrogant, dominating man.

At the studio he worked at a tremendous pace; a thousand things to do, not enough time to do them in. And yet he looked down on the work. He'd get out of it as quickly as possible. Mr. Hackett might take his next play. Or Belasco. The theater pages of the newspapers would talk about an American Ibsen.

He got ready to sign a new contract with the studio. The lawyers said he must sign his real name this time. He seemed almost in pain, as if giving up for the moment something precious, then picked up the pen and signed his full name.

The business office looked on him icily. He had made two

reels out of *Enoch Arden*—that was something not easy to forget. And he had made a picture out of that "Pippa" thing—that was hardest of all to forget. And now, the business office heard, he was going to make a picture from another poem—this time something called "The Bells" by Edgar Allan Poe. The business office said there was something fundamentally wrong with the man. Make good, exciting one-reel pictures, said the business office. Griffith said that one reel was not time enough to tell a story. The two forces clashed.

Rival companies were telling stories, but their stories were preposterous, he thought. "All of them end in a silly chase," he said. On the other hand, he did not realize that fundamentally his stories had the same basic element. He put the heroine in extreme peril, and then, at the last moment, rescued the distressed maiden.

He was, however, doing things that none of the other directors were attempting: the moving camera, new ways of lighting, cutting the film so that two lines of action could be portrayed at the same time without confusing the audience.

The success of a film was measured by how many prints were needed to fill the calls that came in from exhibitors. The average number was fifteen. Soon his pictures were selling twenty-five. The business office looked on him as a boy might who has bought from a pet shop a nice, promising dog, which is turning into a lion. What to do with him? That was the question. If he didn't sell so many prints, the problem would be simple. On top of this he was growing more and more arrogant. And, more and more, he kept his own counsel. Part of the time the business office didn't even know what he was making. He used no scenarios, and he told the actors only enough for them to interpret the action, the mood, and the feeling of the scene they were to play.

The business office tried to get from him what he was doing. "Just experimenting," said the maddening man. The business office set spies—mostly actors—to report what the fool was up to. They came back defeated. The more they watched him, the more confused they became.

Meanwhile, Griffith went on turning out the greatest money-makers on the market. He worked at a furious rate; he never seemed to tire. The other directors "ran through" a scene a time or two, then made it. He rehearsed his cast until the players were ready to drop. Nothing but perfection suited him. So furiously did he work, so great was his energy, that he was turning out two one-reel pictures a week. They were not all distinguished, but they were the best being made. He knew this and took advantage of it. He seemed to like to quarrel with the business office. It was as if, subconsciously, he held them guilty for his failure to sell the things he was writing.

The strange friendship between him and Mack Sennett continued—Griffith, cold, aloof, intellectual; Mack Sennett, the tobacco-chewing former ironworker who thought that reading was a waste of time. Now and then Mack opined that he would like to be a director and make funny pictures about policemen. Griffith again told him that the dignity of the law must be upheld.

"I've got more ideas on the subject," said the unsinkable Mack. "I want to put a bunch of pretty girls in the picture."

"You'd better put an idea into your picture. All my stories have something fundamental in them."

"There's something fundamental about a pretty girl," said Mack, chewing his tobacco thoughtfully.

Griffith's love of art was deep and sincere; the shoddy aroused his scorn. One of the measuring rods used by the studios, as an example of a successful scene, was one that had been issued early in film history. It was called "The Fifty Foot Kiss." It showed two favorite comedians—May Irwin and John C. Rice—engaged in the longest and most fantastic bit of low comedy that had come along. Other directors spoke admiringly of the scene. But not Griffith. "Why didn't they make it a hundred feet long? That would make it twice as good, wouldn't it?" he said scornfully. "A film," he continued, expounding his philosophy of picture making, "is a cooperative effort between the director and the audience. A director shows a bit of human emotion; the audience fills in the rest. The better the film, the greater the cooperation between director and audience."

Another scene from the old Mutoscope days that picture people talked about was Fred Ott's sneeze. "Anybody could pose for the scene and anybody could direct it," he said in his lordly way.

The grip motion pictures were beginning to have was amazing; the little nickelodeon had suddenly blossomed out as a respectable theater. Griffith and others were bringing selective audiences into the theater. The "great unwashed," who had kept the nickelodeon going, were now attending the movies, and so were the denizens of the upper social and financial brackets. Suddenly the intelligentsia discovered the movies. They began to write in ecstatic terms about the "art of the cinema"; not only this but they turned out poems praising it to the sky. The movies had gone through many trying situations, so stood up under this new one. In truth, never had such an overwhelming change of entertainment habit come into the lives of the American people as Griffith and his contemporaries were bringing about.

Interviewers came to talk to him. He told them little about

himself, except that he was the son of Colonel Griffith of Kentucky. He misled them about his age and his background. He became self-conscious that he hadn't even gotten into high school but intimated that he had attended the University of Kentucky. In fact, it cannot be set down that he, at that time, had ever seen the place. The interviewers asked him his theory of movie entertainment. He didn't want to puff up something in which he didn't have his heart, so he developed a kind of jargon. The movies, he said, were a plastic art; their very heart and core was beauty. "What is beauty?" he would ask solemnly. "It is the wind rippling golden wheat." "It is the smile on a baby's face." "It is the secret mirror that every human being has in his heart into which he looks and sees something greater than himself." They were lovely sentences; the only catch was that they didn't make sense, and defined nothing.

He hinted more things than he actually said. If the interviewers wanted to form their own conclusions, that was all right with him. He never contradicted anything that appeared in the papers or magazines. All he wanted was publicity for his stars and his pictures. When his plays were produced, then he would welcome personal publicity.

The result of all this was that people were coming to the movie theaters. That was the important thing. Also, as a result, the theater touring companies and the stock companies were beginning to suffer. Actors no longer slipped off to a film studio with a turned-up collar and a pulled-down hat. There was talk of how much "pictures" were paying—enchanting words. Motion pictures were being treated with more respect; hardly anyone now called them "the flickers."

And these days, as he worked and experimented, he made the discovery that, in close-ups, the success of the "shot" was not dependent on the actor, but on what the actor was doing, what the camera revealed, and how the shot fitted into the mood of the story. In other words, he could put almost any actor in the scene and have a successful picture if the "shot" was right. To this "close-up" he added what he called a "long shot." He began to combine the two, with an intermediate shot in between. The effect was magical. But he kept the secret to himself. Sooner or later other directors would find out, but until then it was his child.

The days went along. His prodigious energy continued. Nearly every picture he released had some innovation, some bit of technique no other picture had. His stories ran to one class—the faithful "last-minute rescue"—the very kind he had been so contemptuous of at first. A change came over him: he began to search for historical stories dealing with social themes —"big stories," he called them. In addition, he was beginning to like stories that had scenes of violence.

He thought of war. The impression the aftermath of the Civil War had made on him was deep. He thought, from time to time, of the face of Christ he had seen that morning. War and Christ—those two were often in his mind.

His idea of the kind of girl an audience wanted to see was quite opposite from the one the theater chose to present. On the spoken stage a girl could be much older, much more mature, and much plumper than the one he wanted to put into his pictures. He believed that a stage star could not survive a close-up, so he selected young, demure girls to be his leading ladies. He was right. Movie audiences wanted 'em young and unsophisticated—and this was exactly what he was giving them. The demand for the Mary Pickford and the Lillian Gish and Dorothy Gish type of girl went up. He was the only director supplying this kind of appeal; the exhibitors knew this and pounded at his doors. Any other director would have been delighted, but Griffith looked on his success as a private acknowledgment that he had not succeeded where it counted.

Audiences who watched the fleeting shadows on the screen wanted to know the real names of the people, where they lived, their love affairs. Griffith had been putting the names of the cast on the screen and now letters came flooding into the studio.

The business office wanted Griffith himself to put his name on his pictures, for, in the trade, he had become well known. The exhibitors talked of a "Griffith picture" and, what was more, wanted to book it. The chief owner of Biograph sent for Griffith to come to his office which was in an uptown building. Once Griffith would have rushed there as fast as he could go, but now he was becoming independent.

Finally he got to the office.

There was some preliminary conversation, then the manager said, "We want you to put your name on your films."

This was the last thing in the world he wanted—to advertise to the world he had not made a success of the thing he wanted to do.

"I'll put the names of the cast, but not mine."

An argument followed; finally he gave in. "All right, I'll put it on."

He left.

When his next picture was released, his name was on it, exactly as he had agreed, but it was cut down to D. W. Griffith. He would save his full name for his plays.

One evening, as Cora served the dinner, she was ill at ease; something was on her mind. Finally she spoke: "Mr. David, I got somethin' to tell you. I got to go an' leave you."

"You mean the little one?"

"Yes. I've been so happy wukking for you. I feel so bad I got to go."

"I feel bad to have you go, Cora," he said sincerely.

They talked of other things, then she said with pride: "I got a white doctah. I am only a poor colored woman, but I like to have high-class people around me."

He was touched. "I'll tell you what I'm going to do, Cora. I'm going to give you fifty dollars for the big event."

She was speechless, so delighted, so overwhelmed was she. "Mr. David," she finally managed to say, "I don't know when I ever see anybody I feel so good toward. You're my people, Mr. David."

"You're my people, too," he said warmly—this man who so much of the time was impersonal and aloof.

When Cora finished her work, she gathered up her few possessions and left. He sat thinking about her for a few moments, then got out his writing material.

CHAPTER 6

HE MAKES A FOUR-REELER

AFTER CORA LEFT HE BECAME DISCONTENTED with his apartment and moved to the Hotel Astor. He was now part of Broadway, the world he would soon be writing for. He liked to stalk through the lobby in his lordly way and have people ask who he was. He told the hotel help he was a playwright, and encouraged people to believe he was one. Paul Armstrong, the dramatist of the day, was living at the hotel. Whenever Griffith saw him in the lobby, he would go up to him and talk animatedly, looking out of the corner of his eyes to see if people were watching.

As money began to come in, he found he liked the feel of it. It was the mark of the successful. He started to spend freely; more would come in. As soon as he had enough to feel secure, he would throw over this whole miserable business.

A daring idea came to him. He would make a four-reel motion picture.

But what to make the picture about? His mind went to his early days, as it so often did when he was working out an idea, and recalled a story his sister Mattie had read to him from the Apocrypha—the story of Judith. He had been thrilled then; did it have the same power? He reread that sanguinary saga:

Nebuchadnezzar, the Babylonian war king, was winning right and left; the world would soon be his—so he thought. He sent his general—Holofernes—to tear down the temple in Jerusalem. And Holofernes just about had his way. The people he was attacking were soon starving. Their end seemed not far away. But there was a charming widow who lived in Bethulia hard by—Judith of Bethulia she was called. She said in effect, "Let me see this vain man. I'll twist his nose." She dressed herself in dazzling raiment, took her maid, and went to the enemy camp and asked to see Holofernes. When the guard demanded why she wanted to see Holofernes she said, "I have something to tell him"—which proved to be an exceedingly mild statement. When she was led before the great warrior, he was gruff and suspicious and said, "What is it you have to tell me?"

"I want to speak of love," said Judith, blushing becomingly.

"Well," said the mighty warrior.

As might be expected, the general succumbed to her beauty; in fact, he was so delighted with her charms and witty conversation that he ordered a great banquet to be given in her honor. This turned out to be a mistake in judgment, for he became intoxicated and lay down on the floor, completely pie-eyed. This was the moment Judith had been waiting for. "I will dance for you," she said. She did dance for him for a few minutes, then gave a leap and cut off his head; she danced with this, performing all kinds of graceful steps. Finally she handed the head to her maid, who did not really want it. The death of Holofernes gave the Jews confidence and they fell upon the enemy and killed them in great numbers. Judith had won for her people. It was a bloody story of sex and war, but, as Griffith reread it, he liked it. The public would, too.

He told Billy Bitzer his idea. "Billy, I've got a tremendous idea! It's to make a four-reel picture."

"It cannot be done, Mr. Greeffith. The business office will think it is crazy and will give you no money."

"I'll go ahead, anyway."

"Dot would be badt. What is it the picture about?" asked Billy.

"It's a story from the writings at the time of the Bible. Judith of Bethulia is the heroine. A wicked king has been oppressing her people. She goes to a great banqueting hall, gets the king inebriated, cuts off his head, and dances with it."

"She dances mit der king's head?" asked the shocked man.

"Yes, on a platter. It will be a wonderful scene."

"Do peoples want to see a girl dancing mit a head on a plate?"

"They will the way I'll handle it."

Billy studied the man he admired so greatly. "For anybody else I would say it is crazy and I t'ink maybe it is for you."

"You'll like it when you see it."

"I neffer want to see anybody dancing mit a head on a plate."

Griffith was alarmed. "You'll stay with me anyway, won't you, Billy? You won't run off and join some other director, will you?"

"I will stay mit you, no matter how crazy you can be."

"Billy, did you ever stop to think that most of the people who have done new and different things have been considered crazy? Did you ever stop to think of that?"

"Yes, I have t'ink of it. But maybe dis time peoples are right."

Griffith had made up his mind; he was going to let nothing discourage him.

The tension between Griffith and the officers of Biograph had been growing. Why didn't he make the kind of pictures the exhibitors wanted? they asked. One-reel pictures were sold in advance, on a regular booking schedule, yet the man wanted to make two-reelers.

His players had become known as the "Griffith Actors"

and were the best-known group of film players in America. He had taken them when they were unknown and made them national figures. He had command of them, as a father might have of his children. The jealousy between them was endless. Owen Moore—the gay-hearted Irishman—had fallen in love with Mary Pickford; the two had quarrels and spats and came to him with their troubles. And the jealous ones came to him with their troubles, too. And he settled them as a father might. His control of his players was almost hypnotic. They would do as he wished, even if some of the time his solutions didn't seem to make sense. But in some mysterious way things worked out right. His pictures were a succession of triumphs. Actors began to boast of being a Griffith player. No lowered eyes now. They even talked of the "old days" when they'd worn a wig so their friends wouldn't recognize them.

His players were Lillian Gish, Dorothy Gish, Blanche Sweet, Robert Harron, Mae Marsh, Henry B. Walthall, Jack Pickford, Owen Moore, James Kirkwood, Donald Crisp, Mary Pickford—and faithful Billy Bitzer.

Sundays he set aside for himself. Most of such a day he spent either reading or writing; now and then he went to the Methodist Church, the church he had been brought up in, the one his mother attended. In the early days his mother had told him she wished he would become a minister. So important was the church in Crestwood that when he became an actor his name was taken off the church roll. His mother had always been sensitive about this disgrace, and when he came to see her, she mentioned it, still hurt.

These Sundays in the hotel he felt he really lived. He could do exactly as he wished; no quarrels with the business office, no one to tell him he was not making the kind of pictures the exhibitors wanted. And he could swing his Indian clubs when-

ever he wished. They had become more and more a part of his
life, along with his dumb bar bells and weights. They helped
make him strong, he believed, and kept him healthy. He liked
to swing them, dressed only in his underclothes, now and then
taking a healthy, deep breath and giving a satisfied grunt.

On this day the telephone rang and when he answered, the
operator said that "Cora" wanted to talk to him. "Could I
come up an' see you, Mr. David?"

Maybe she was in trouble. Colored people were always
getting into trouble and coming to their white friends. Well,
it was nice to have a friend who was as loyal as Cora.

"You certainly can, Cora," he said heartily. "I'm doing my
exercises, but you come on, anyway."

There she was when he opened the door—that unusually
black face, that broad body, the fine white teeth. She gave a
little start at seeing his thin, angular body in his underwear,
but in a moment her embarrassment was gone. In her arms was
a bundle of flounces and ribbons; a small black face stared out.

He was delighted; it was an honor for her to bring the baby
for him to see. Cora and David talked about the child and
how she was getting along, then she said, "Mr. David, I got a
surprise for you. This is David G. Hawkins! He named for
you."

He and Cora laughed and talked in the easy way they had
when he had been living in the cramped little flat.

At last the surprise visit was over and Cora left with little
"Davie" in her arms. After she was gone, he felt lonesome;
here had been a touch of the Old South in the days when the
Griffiths had a plantation and servants, before the family had
been ruined by the Reconstruction. But the mood did not last
long. Picking up his Indian clubs, he began to exercise again,
drawing fresh breaths and giving little grunts of satisfaction.

Then he took a bath, pulled out his papers, and began to write, the fine fire of creation blazing in him.

Something new came into his life.

From the very first, in order to save money, many scenes had been taken outdoors. And this still held. But the background and settings were chosen more carefully. The New Jersey Palisades would hardly pass for the Alps and a stuffed turkey would hardly pass as a fighting eagle.

California—golden California!—where outdoor pictures could be taken all winter long. That was the solution. Small companies of picture makers had gone out; their expenses had been whacked in half. And so "Mr. D. W." prepared to take his children and go to that heavenly spot.

He made two pictures but his mind was on his "big" production that was going to thrill the public and put America far ahead in the picture race. Pictures were being imported from France and Italy; in many ways they were better than American pictures. One reason for this was that the foreign pictures were not hampered by the "Trust" that had got a stranglehold on American pictures. A silent warfare had been going on for four years—the Trust against the small independent producers. Gangs of ruffians had been hired by the Trust to break up any picture company that did not use their cameras and pay the license fees demanded. Men posing as "extras" came on the set; suddenly they would swoop down on the camera, knocking it to pieces and exposing the film. Not only this, but there had been mysterious fires in the laboratories; in truth, a reign of terror had been going on. Yet Griffith had survived. In some amazing way he had managed to make pictures. Now, in California, he would not have so many problems to contend with—and he could make outdoor pictures all winter. It was heaven, indeed.

At such a driving pace did he go that three days after he and his players arrived in Hollywood he was making a picture. His confidence in himself was unlimited. He considered himself a genius. He would make pictures such as had never been made before. He believed this, and he made others believe it.

The other companies, working in Hollywood, did little or no rehearsing. They "ran through" a scene a time or two, then began to crank. But this did not do for Griffith; he rehearsed his players until they hated him—for the time being. None of the cameramen knew how fast to turn, so they counted how many times the handle went around in a minute. Sometimes, when the picture was on the screen, it went by with dizzying rapidity; sometimes it moved slowly and uncertainly. But audiences did not hoot. America was becoming "picture conscious"; this was the most superb kind of entertainment America had ever known. People were flocking to the theaters. Audiences wanted more and more to know about the actors they saw on the screen. The picture companies reversed themselves: they now sent out publicity boasting how many letters their stars got each week.

There always had been a bond between the aloof D. W. Griffith and the heavy-handed, tobacco-chewing Mack Sennett, and so, as soon as he got to Los Angeles, Griffith hired a car and driver and went to Glendale to see his friend. He felt sorry for Mack, for Mack was a likable fellow but was approaching the picture business from the wrong angle. He should not make a mistake in the business which, every day, was becoming more competitive. He should be making "worth-while" pictures.

He expected to find his old friend in some fenced-off back

lot doing the best he could with the few dollars he could scrape up. The car stopped before a high board fence. There was a door and there was a gate. A uniformed guard looked him over. Griffith stared at the man. Why, he himself had never had anything like that!

"I want to see Mr. Sennett."

"What's your name?" asked the guard.

Griffith told him.

The guard mumbled into a telephone, listened to a reply, then opened the door and motioned for Griffith to enter. "Take him to the boss's office," the man said to another uniformed guard, and Griffith set off across the lot behind the new man.

Griffith gazed about him in astonishment. Here was a going studio, a very busy and complicated one. Here were trick cars, trick furniture, trick sets. Carpenters pounded, plumbers worked, a medley of people in grease paint and wearing outrageous clothes hurried past, paying not the least attention to him. Bathing beauties, in hardly any clothes at all, sauntered by, twirling gay parasols over their shoulders. As much as Griffith knew about studios, he knew little or nothing about the crazy land of comedy.

Griffith arrived at Mack's office.

Big, lumbering Mack Sennett—who always seemed to be wearing a hat—seized Griffith's hand. "How are you, D. W.? Welcome to California. What're you here for?"

"I'm going to make pictures."

"The same goody-goody kind?"

"I think they have a social significance."

Mack smiled at the quaint idea.

"My new one," said Griffith defensively, "is from Bible times."

"It is?" said the astonished Mack. "Do you think people are interested in Bible stories?"

"They always have been."

"I'd rather put my money on funny policemen."

"We'll see," said Griffith loftily.

The subject was dropped and the two began to talk of what was already called the days when Mack had been a comedian in *The Curtain Pole*. And now Mack spoke of the time when Griffith had had the fight with the eagle, laughing uproariously at what now seemed an exceedingly amusing event. But Griffith did not laugh; he wanted to forget it. He spoke, instead, of the stories he had sold to Biograph and gave the impression, without quite saying so, that he was selling things to magazines. "How did you get the name Keystone?" he asked, delicately changing the subject.

"I got it when I was workin' for you, back in New York. I was walkin' to the Pennsylvania Station with Mr. Kessel. He was going to take a train to Philadelphia and took a time-table out of his pocket and I saw the drawing and the word 'Keystone,' and I said to myself, 'If that's good enough for a big company like the Pennsylvania Railroad, it's good enough for me.' That's the way I hooked onto it."

They talked a while longer, then Mack said hospitably, "Have lunch with me."

"Thanks. I'd like to."

"Do you remember how we used to bring our lunches in a shoe box?" asked Mack.

The two continued to visit until lunch was ready to be served in Mack's office. Two of his comedians came in, were introduced, and sat down at the table. A waiter arrived with a bowl of soup and started to place it in front of Griffith, then changed his mind, drank it himself, placed the empty bowl in front of Griffith, and went on about his work. A sandwich was passed and when Griffith took it, the sandwich began to twitch and jerk. Griffith put down the rubber sandwich and managed to smile. But not Mack and the comedians; what they had seen was normal conduct for a sandwich, their manner implied.

The crazy, impossible meal went on.

"I want to show you my latest Keystone cops," said Mack when the meal was over, and took him to the projection room and ran off a comedy. In one scene a comedian started to shave; for some obscure reason a lion was immediately behind him, but the comedian did not see him. Reaching behind him, he got hold of the lion's tail, and, thinking it was a shaving brush, began to lather his face.

"Ain't that the funniest scene you ever saw?" said Mack, slapping his mighty leg with his heavy hand. "That'll knock 'em out of their seats!"

"I'm sure it will," said Griffith with as much enthusiasm as he could manage.

A bathing beauty in the picture came out with a dog and started to lead it behind her. But the leash was dropped and, by mistake, she picked up a rope and began to lead the lion around, thinking it was her dog.

"Ain't that wonderful?" said Mack, again slapping his leg and roaring with laughter.

"It certainly is," said Griffith weakly. On the way back to the office he asked, "Is there any market for pictures like the one you showed me?"

"Is there! My business office tells me that my pictures are making more money than yours."

Griffith was stunned. "But they're not significant," he said defensively.

"A picture that makes money is significant," said Mack.

The time came for Griffith to go. Mack called one of the workmen. "Tom, you're not doing anything. Get a car and take Mr. Griffith to the Alexandria Hotel."

"Yes, sir," said the man respectfully.

Farewells were said and the unsuspecting Griffith got in. The car ran a few yards, then began to buck and pitch; there was an explosion, and the car fell apart. Griffith leaped out, shocked. The people on the lot, suspecting something, had gathered around and now laughed heartily at what, to them, was a delicious bit of comedy, involving what they called a "breakaway" car.

Griffith was put into Mack's own luxurious car, with a driver, and finally was on his way. He thought of what Mack had said of how much money his pictures were making and how little, by comparison, his own were making. Well, that would soon change. The success of *Judith of Bethulia* would startle fun-loving Mack.

One day in the studio word was brought to him that Mrs. Loos wanted to see him. He got up promptly and went toward her; on his head was a great flapping sombrero, tied with a black shoestring. Here, waiting in a little railed-off place, were Mrs. Loos and a girl. He approached rapidly and extended his hand to Mrs. Loos. "It's a pleasure to meet 'A. Loos,' " he said in his impressive southern way, with a deep bow. "But I always thought you were a man!"

"I'm not 'A. Loos,' " said the mother. "This is 'A. Loos.' "

Griffith looked at the girl, stunned. "Are you the one I've been buying stories from?"

"Under the O. Henry influence, I signed them 'A. Loos.' I was a schoolgirl and I thought I was being very professional."

He continued to look at his prize contributor, hardly believing. "I never dreamed it was a girl. I tell you," he said sincerely, "writing is a great gift. So few have it."

There were many calls for him, people coming with this demand or that, but he continued to talk, still trying to adjust himself to a new way of thinking. At last Mrs. Loos and her daughter left, and Griffith returned to his directing.

Griffith was exceedingly careful in selecting his players. They must look the part, and they must feel the part. Actors were now—so much had the attitude toward motion pictures changed—eager to be chosen; with reasonable luck, they would become national figures.

For some time he had been watching Blanche Sweet and now chose her for the Jewish Judith, which must have surprised her, for she was a blonde. For Holofernes he selected Henry B. Walthall, also seemingly a strange choice, for Walthall was a sensitive, gentle man, not at all the warrior type. Lillian Gish was the Little Mother in Israel. She was to go among the people, begging water for her baby. Strange choices, but he believed these players had possibilities and that he could bring them out. He would soon know.

He selected Chatsworth Park as the place to make the picture and here it was started in June 1912. The cast had to get up at five in the morning, go by streetcar, but not all the way, for the streetcar did not quite make it to Chatsworth Park. A hay wagon met them at the end of the line and jolted off to Jerusalem.

Most directors took scenes in the order most convenient; sometimes the end of the story would be the first photographed. But Griffith did not follow this order; he directed in sequence; in this way the actors knew what they were portraying and could put the right feeling into the scene.

The hot summer! The heavy oriental costumes! But the cast continued faithfully under the inspired director. At last the exteriors were finished and the cast was taken back to New York where the interiors were made in the Biograph Studio in the Bronx. Here Holofernes got what he so richly deserved and Judith danced with the head.

Griffith set about the cutting and the editing of his master-piece. It was finished February 23, 1913, and he invited Jeremiah J. Kennedy, with whom he had had so many clashes, to view the new epoch-making film in the studio's tiny projection room. Nothing so ambitious, so pretentious, had been made in America; it would establish Biograph as the leading picture studio in the world, and it would send Griffith's name soaring.

The tall, cold, stone-faced Kennedy arrived.

"I think you're going to like it, Mr. Kennedy," said Griffith effusively. "It's something new in pictures and ought to do a great deal for us."

"I hope so, the way things are going. How long is it?"

"Four reels."

" 'Four reels?' " repeated the shocked man. "We can't sell a four-reel picture. The exhibitors have no arrangements for handling a film of that length."

"Can't we put it out as a 'special attraction'?"

"No. The booking and distributing systems are arranged in such a way that this can't be done. You have wasted our money."

"But, Mr. Kennedy, it's something new!"

"We don't want something new, as you call it. We want pictures that can be handled and distributed without upsetting our entire system."

There was a silence.

"I've looked up the cost sheet," continued Mr. Kennedy,

"and I find the picture has cost us $36,000. That makes it the most expensive picture ever produced."

"I think it will pay off, Mr. Kennedy."

There was another painful silence, then Mr. Kennedy said: "Why didn't you consult us? You wouldn't tell us; you worked in secret; we had confidence in you and now this . . ."

"I wanted to make an artistic picture. I couldn't very well explain what I had in mind. I kept changing it as I went along, getting new ideas and adding to it."

"Why didn't you tell us your ideas? I happen to know a little about the film business."

"I know you do, Mr. Kennedy. But this dealt with art."

"It also dealt with money. It won't fit into our standard weekly output, it won't fit into anything. We can't release it. It'll have to go into the vault."

"Maybe, when you see the picture, you'll change your mind."

They went into the projection room.

The picture was run off.

"I haven't changed my mind in the least," said Mr. Kennedy when the ordeal was over. "Dancing with that head—it would shock audiences."

"I think they would like it, Mr. Kennedy."

"I don't."

Mr. Kennedy left and Griffith was alone in defeat.

But he wasn't defeated, not quite. He had had an idea for a story about the War Between the States, dealing especially with the Reconstruction period. He began to think about it again.

He was now thirty-nine.

CHAPTER 7

HE MAKES THE BIRTH OF
A NATION

Judith of Bethulia WAS HELD IN THE VAULTS
for a year, then released—not as a "special feature," but as a
unit in the Trust's routine weekly output. Handled this way—
as part of the service for which the exhibitors paid a fee—
the company could not ask a higher price for the film. As a result it was considered a financial failure and Griffith was looked
on as a director who could not be depended on. The public
did not want "multiple-reel pictures," the Trust said. In this
the Trust was a trifle in error; the public wanted them very
much, indeed. The Trust, however, stubbornly refused to
change its policy and soon was in trouble, and finally failed.
Meantime, the public was eating up "multiple-reel pictures,"
but the Trust was too dead to see the depressing spectacle.

Griffith left Biograph and joined Mutual, with a special contract with Harry E. Aitken, its president, which allowed him
to make any kind of picture he wanted. Griffith rejoiced. He
was now, in effect, his own master. He would not be harried
by the box office. He arrived in Los Angeles February 14, 1914,
on fire to make the kind of picture he wanted to make without
the business office having a hand on his shoulder. And with
him, just as eager as Griffith, was faithful Billy Bitzer.

Griffith had in process of production, cutting, printing, and
release three pictures which must be finished before he began

The One. He tore into them; they promised to be money-makers.

While nominally supervising these productions for Mutual, Griffith was secretly at work on his new and inspiring story. He was hiring extras and costumes. A war was preparing in Europe; the one he was getting ready to film was more real to him than the one across the ocean.

He had always spoken contemptuously of picture making. He would say to Billy Bitzer, "Well, let's get to work and grind out another sausage." But he had no such reflection on the new picture he was just starting; it would tell the truth about the neglected South.

The story principle, which he had established at the very beginning, was still in effect: the Griffith last-minute rescue. He had added to this bare bones the matter of social importance. Poor Dolly, in *The Adventures of Dolly*, had been rescued from her barrel at the last possible moment. Even in *Judith of Bethulia* the Jews had been saved by Judith with her platter. But he no longer wanted what he called "family situations"; he wanted a story that dealt with masses of people under stress, even with the fate of nations. He had always had this social consciousness; now he could make others aware of it.

He had seen a stage play entitled *The Clansman* by the Reverend Thomas E. Dixon, of North Carolina. The play was tawdry, but in it was an idea—the condition of the South after the Union armies had retired in victory. The idea had been stowed away in his mind; he reread the book. He read also another book of the Reverend Mr. Dixon—*The Leopard's Spots*—and decided to use part of this story in the general plot. He would depict the aftermath of the war and would show what had happened to thousands of southerners who had lost everything, like his father. This would be no pitiful four-reeler; it would be the biggest, the most important picture ever made.

He told Harry Aitken what he wanted to do. Aitken said that he knew the mind of the directors of his company and that they would never agree to put up the sum needed—$50,000. A blow, indeed. After some discussion Griffith suggested they form their own company and produce the picture. Aitken agreed to this and said he would be personally responsible for the $50,000. It was a wonderful, breathtaking moment. Griffith—who did not think in small terms—named the company the Epoch Film Corporation.

The time had come! He could produce, could be his own master. He would do big things.

He had two other films to finish, but secretly he was working on the story of the South. As usual, he had the outline in his head; there would be no scenario. He would take the scenes in the order that seemed best. His imagination leaped; his mind soared; he had wings. He would depict the most dramatic events that had taken place in the War Between the States. He would show the Battle of Petersburg; he would show Sherman's march to the sea; the burning of Atlanta; the assassination of President Lincoln. He would show the Negroes being led by "carpetbaggers" from the North, and he would show how law and order were restored by the Night Riders.

He laid the evils of Reconstruction on two leaders of the Republican party: Senator Charles Sumner, of Massachusetts, and Congressman Thaddeus Stevens of Pennsylvania. Supporters of Stevens pointed out that he lived for years with a Negro woman in Washington, D.C. But it must also be pointed out that he did not marry her; the reason for this, it was said, was because he was afraid he would lose social caste in Washington.

Who were to be his actors? Well, he would use the Griffith Players, and so he selected Lillian Gish, Mae Marsh, Henry B. Walthall, Robert Harron; Donald Crisp was to play General Grant, Raoul Walsh was to play John Wilkes Booth, and Erich von Stroheim was to have a small part. And there were to be lesser players. (Mary Pickford had joined another company and was not available.)

The building of the sets and the laying out of the battle-fields were begun; a whole city must be built—later to be burned. Eighteen thousand soldiers had to be arranged for—men to fight for the North and men to fight for the South. And they must have not only uniforms, but also horses. An unexpected difficulty arose. A war in Europe was imminent and the quarreling nations were buying horses in this country. He had to have horses, come what might, so he went into the market and bid against England, France, Italy, and Russia. And he must have shells that would explode, and these he bid for; they were harmless, but otherwise the same as the armies were to use. And vast quantities of cotton goods for the Ku Klux Klan—these had to be secured against foreign bidding.

His plans mounted; his ambition soared.

"Billy," he said, "I'm going to take battle scenes at night."

" 'Battle scenes at night'?" repeated Billy Bitzer. "It cannot be done, Mr. Greeffith. It is not known how."

"We'll learn. Remember, battle scenes at night. That's what I want."

"Ve vill do it, Mr. Greeffith," said Billy.

Rehearsals started. He had always been demanding of his

cast; now he was more so than ever. They complained, but he pushed them on, sometimes even bullying them.

Expenses mounted.

The actor-killing rehearsals continued day after day. He carried everything in his head; not a scrap of paper to guide him. The days he had spent working on his history of the South were now yielding dividends. He knew the war as did few people. But it was from the southern point of view. For six weeks the rehearsals continued; no scene was too small to be rushed over; no scene so big that it could not be improved. He rehearsed the shooting of President Lincoln twenty-two times.

Finally the great day came. The camera turned for the first time—and the day was July 4, 1914.

A strip of land had been rented from private owners and closed off; here the battle scenes were rehearsed and then made; there was no retake. And then the ride of the Clansmen was made. Billy Bitzer staked his camera down so as to get the effect of the horses passing over him; and this they did, indeed, as he lay on the ground in the dust raised by their thundering feet. In fact, one of the horses crashed into the camera and broke it. Hastily the camera was patched up and the fierce, demoniac ride continued.

It became a struggle to pay the cast, especially the extras—and there were 16,000 of them. Also there was the matter of supplying them lunch on the set. He himself had to go to the store that was making up the boxes and ask the store to trust him. It agreed to.

No sooner was one problem solved than another came to take its place. But he kept the camera turning; the picture was going into the box. He worked furiously; no writing in secret now.

Mr. Aitken came to him. "Griffith, I see on the office memorandum you want more money. Haven't you got enough?"

"No, Mr. Aitken. I'll have to have more."

"You've spent all the money set aside for the picture."

"Things have been against me, Mr. Aitken. The war has made a big difference. I'll need $50,000 more."

Mr. Aitken looked at him, aghast. "We haven't got it and we can't get it. Finish up the picture and we'll salvage what we can."

"The picture would be botched. I couldn't do that, Mr. Aitken."

"Then you'll have to do it alone. There will be no more money."

Griffith was stunned. The picture was half completed—no more money.

It was a black night, but he was not defeated.

Work was stopped. Griffith went to his friends and asked for money—a bitter experience for such a proud and haughty man.

"I haf friendts undt I vill ask dem," said Billy Bitzer.

"I have friends, too," said John D. Barry, his secretary and office manager. "I have a well-to-do one in Pasadena. I'll ask him."

A day or two later Barry came into Griffith's office, his face beaming, his eyes shining. He held up a check. "Mr. Griffith, I've got $700."

For a moment Griffith could not speak. "God is on our side," he said, touched.

There appeared on the set the Reverend Thomas Dixon, tall and lean and sallow. Actors in make-up and in Civil War costumes were waiting to be rehearsed; they stared at the visitor. Who was he? Griffith went quickly to meet him. The actors stared at this, too, for they knew that their director did not like to be interrupted in a scene. After the greetings were over, the distinguished author came directly to the point. "D. W., y'know—"

Griffith caught the tone. "Excuse me," he said hastily; "let's walk over there where we can be alone. I think it will be better," he added in a notable understatement.

"You know," continued Dixon when they withdrew, "you agreed to pay me $2,500 for my book and play. I dislike to speak of this, but I haven't got anything yet."

Griffith was embarrassed and ill at ease. "I'm kind of low on money just now, Mr. Dixon. Could you wait awhile? I'll pay you, you can depend on that."

"I feel I have the right to expect it now. You led me to believe that in the beginning," said the austere visitor.

"I know I did, but unexpected expenses have come up."

There was an embarrassed silence.

"Mr. Dixon, will you accept ten times that amount in stock in our company?"

He didn't know about that, the Reverend Mr. Dixon said; stock deals were always a treacherous business. But the earnest, the persuasive Griffith got him to agree, and finally the Reverend Mr. Dixon left.

The actors were watching the sallow man and they were watching Griffith, but Griffith offered no explanation.

"Who was dot sour apple?" asked the privileged Billy Bitzer.

"An old friend," said Griffith and then, without being too abrupt with Billy, took up his directing.

At last the picture was finished.

So well had he rehearsed—so well had he prepared—that not one battle scene had to be taken over.

All of the picture, including the battle scenes and the ride of the Clansmen, was shot with one camera. That camera has disappeared; no one knows what became of it.

(NOTE: If that camera could be found and put on exhibit in the D. W. Griffith section of the Museum of Modern Art, it would be an outstanding addition. It would bring us close to this great period in American picture making.)

The most famous "still" picture that has ever come out of Hollywood was one involving Lillian Gish and an unknown soldier—unknown, that is, until recently. The still showed Lillian Gish coming out of the hospital in Atlanta; as she came out, a Union soldier, his hands resting wearily on his rifle, sees Lillian and looks at her with such yearning, in such an I-see-an-angel way that it brought down the house. The man was an extra and when the film was over he melted into the California mist. Years later, in fact, recently, it was discovered this immortal was a man named Walter Freeman. (*Author's comment:* I wonder if he is living. I hope so, indeed.)

Then came the cutting. Griffith sat in the little cutting room on a chair with metal legs, hunched over the cutting table, endlessly running the film forward and backward to bring out the contrasts he wished. He seemed always to know what he wanted and he seemed never to tire.

Finally the picture was completed; it had cost $110,000— a staggering sum.

From Mae Marsh, in a letter to the author:

You ask what salary we got in *The Birth of a Nation*. He was driven for money, but there was not a week we were not paid. I got $35 a week. In *Intolerance* I got $85. After the release of *Intolerance* and the attention the picture attracted, I joined the newly formed Goldwyn Pictures Corporation at $3,000 a week. That was the way things went in early Hollywood.

Griffith was ready to show the picture to the business office. The twelve reels were run off—it was the longest picture that had ever been made. The businessmen regarded it coldly; it would not fit into the program.

"Sell it as a special feature," said the weary man.

"Pictures are not sold that way."

"This picture is different."

"It has to be sold like any picture."

The businessmen showed him where he was wrong.

Whatever happened, Mutual owned half of the picture; Griffith, his friends, and immediate backers, owned the rest.

The picture had been made in secret; only Griffith and the cast knew what it was about. The picture was inflammatory, people said; it was propaganda against the Negroes. Griffith heard the rumors but could not accept them. His was a fair and impartial retelling of the aftermath of the Civil War.

Talk mounted. Politicians, with their eyes on the Negro vote, helped arouse racial excitement. Finally came the night the picture was to open. As publicity horsemen were hired to put on Ku Klux Klan regalia and ride through Central Park (later known as Pershing Square) toward the theater, and there, at Clune's Auditorium, in Los Angeles, the picture opened, February 8, 1915.

So great was the excitement that the police had to patrol the streets. Inside, the picture was flashing across the screen in such scenes as had never before been witnessed in the world. Many of the Hollywood-trained people knew they had come in contact with greatness.

After the show, Griffith met Billy Bitzer outside. "How did you like it, Billy?"

"It is goot, like I always tell you it vas."

"How did you like the night shots?"

"They are goot, like I tell you they would be," said Billy.

Griffith rushed to New York with a print for the Reverend Thomas Dixon and a group of exhibitors to see. It was unreeled in a small company projection room. It aroused the hard-bitten exhibitors into a burst of applause—a record-breaking event, if there ever was one. The Reverend Thomas Dixon himself sprang to his feet.

"It's wonderful!" he cried, his voice shaking with emotion. "It's bigger than the title suggests. It should be called *The Birth of a Nation*, for that is exactly what it is!"

"I like the title you suggest," said Griffith, and so did the exhibitors; then and there a new title was born.

Immediately word came that President Wilson wanted to see it. Griffith was particularly eager to know what the President would say, for he had based some of the scenes on Woodrow Wilson's book, *A History of the American People*. A print was taken by messenger to Washington and just one week to a night from the time it opened in Los Angeles it was shown to President Wilson and his family and to members of the Cabinet and their families—the first time the President of the United States had ever asked to "see" a picture. When the picture started to unreel, the guests talked, as people will. One by one they became silent, lost in the sweep of epic events. After a time none spoke, so great was the effect of the story.

When the picture was over, President Wilson sat for some moments, greatly moved. "It's like writing history with lightning," he said.

So much feeling did the film arouse that people in high places said things that can hardly be understood today. Charles W. Eliot, president of Harvard, said: "I want to say that the film presents an extraordinary misrepresentation of the birth of this nation." It was a very telling observation; the only thing the matter was that he had not seen the picture.

The first to seize upon its possibilities was the newly organized Ku Klux Klan, which had been resurrected from the Reconstruction days following the Civil War. In Austin, Texas, the Clansmen put on their robes of white and scarlet, formed in a body at Wooldridge Park, marched down Congress Avenue, turned into Sixth Street, and filled to capacity the Hancock Opera House which the Klan had taken over for the night.

The original Klan had met in 1865 on top of Stone Mountain, near Atlanta, Georgia, under the leadership of General Nathan Bedford Forrest. The present Clansmen in Atlanta organized into a body, some on horseback, some on foot—all dressed in their official ghostlike regalia, and marched down Peachtree. Fiery crosses, carried along the line of march, burned ominously. The Clansmen poured into the theater; those who couldn't get in patrolled the streets. When the picture was over, the men who had seen it were in such a frenzy when they came out that they fired off their pistols.

It was announced that the picture was coming to Boston, the birthplace of Abolition, the city from which William Lloyd Garrison—the first Abolitionist—had thundered. Immediately the city was in arms. Negro preachers and Negro leaders and white teachers and lawyers denounced the film. It should not open. But it did open in April 1915 at Tremont Temple. Four thousand Negroes, led by white supporters, turned out to oppose it. They gathered on the steps of the capitol building, on Beacon Hill, and demanded that the film be suppressed. There were just as many people on the other side, demanding that the film continue. There was a clash. The police could not control the situation; the Boston Fire Department was hastily summoned and came with its hose. The clash promptly became worse. The call went out for medical aid. Two ambulances were required to get the injured to the hospitals.

Governor Walsh threatened Griffith with arrest.

Griffith was bewildered by the storm of protest that swept the country. He was derided on the streets; he got threatening letters and telephone calls. He was attacked by newspapers. He said that he loved Negroes; they said that if the picture represented his love, they did not want it. He had no knack for controversy and got the worst of it. At first he had been proud of the picture; now he did not want to be seen in public and would go to no social function.

Griffith was back in the Hotel Astor, but now he did not have to walk through the lobby to attract attention. He was the man of the hour, the most talked-about man in the entertainment field in America.

The telephone rang. "Mayor Mitchell wants to talk to you."

The mayor of New York!

Griffith could hardly believe his ears.

"I want to see you," said John Purroy Mitchell when he came on the telephone. "A committee has asked me to go with them to your hotel."

What, thought Griffith, could a committee want to talk to him about? Was it some kind of award?

When the door opened, Griffith was surprised to have Mayor Mitchell, one white man, and two Negroes walk in. Introductions were made. Mayor Mitchell came immediately to the point. "We are shocked by your picture. You have done a great injustice to the colored people, and, in all fairness, you should take the picture off."

Griffith was stunned. "What do you think is wrong?" he finally managed to ask.

"You make," said one of the committee, "the Negroes out as heinous, inhuman creatures. Every time a Negro appears in the film, he is a villain."

"The villains are the carpetbaggers," said Griffith when he got possession of himself. "They were white; they led the colored people into the situations I depicted. I must tell you, we have very carefully researched the story and everything shown on the screen happened. You have no right to ask me, on historical grounds, to close the picture, and I will not agree to do so."

"The Negroes never acted that way," said one of the committee harshly. "You have them seizing white girls on the streets and making off with them. That is not true."

"I am afraid it is true," said Griffith, dismayed by the bitterness displayed against him. "You don't realize the impact that the War Between the States made on people. People—Negroes and whites—were not in their right minds. That is what it amounted to."

"I accuse you," said one of the committee, "of being anti-Negro."

"I'm not anti-anybody," said the shocked man. "I'm so overwhelmed by your accusations that I can hardly speak. But I will say this. I grew up with Negroes. I was nursed by a Negro mammy."

The talk grew in heat. Griffith maintained he was innocent; the mayor and the committee maintained he had brought disgrace and humiliation on what one of the committee called "ten million American citizens." Griffith said again that the real culprits were the carpetbaggers; and that the southerners were better friends to the Negroes than the unscrupulous men from the North. Finally it was settled: Griffith agreed to take out the hate-arousing scenes; and this was done. One hundred and seventy scenes were taken out. One thousand three hundred and seventy-four "shots" were left in.

The picture reopened.

Even with the deletions, the situation was so delicate that Pinkerton detectives were placed in the audience to see that there was no disturbance. And there they sat, performance after performance, ready to pounce. But they were not called on and did not have to pounce.

The picture as offered to the public was two hours and forty-five minutes long.

Griffith had suddenly been catapulted into national attention. Some people were calling him a genius; others were denouncing him bitterly. He himself was bewildered by the violence of the feeling that had been aroused against him personally. He went around in a cloud, hardly knowing what to do. The only thing he knew was that he was right and that he had presented a fair treatment of conditions after the war.

He had to guard himself against fanatics who must see him personally and tell him where he was wrong.

The telephone at the Astor rang. "Cora Hawkins is here to see you," the operator said.

He was delighted. How well the two of them had got along together. How well they understood each other.

When he heard the elevator he went out—and there was broad, thick, heavy-waisted, square-faced Cora. With her was a little boy.

"Hello, Cora!" he called heartily. "Come in. I'm glad to see you. Is this little David?"

"How-de-do, Mr. David," said Cora soberly. "Yes, that's my boy. I been tellin' him about you."

"Sit down, Cora. Well, he's a promising-looking boy. I often think of those days on East Thirty-seventh Street, and how you cheered me up when I was low."

"I think of them, too," said Cora in the same sober, reserved way.

They talked, but not in the easy way of old. "A person doesn't know how time races by until he sees an old friend who reminds him of the past," said Griffith. "Well, how're things with you, Cora? I hope everything is going well."

Cora moved uneasily. Something was on her mind.

"Mr. David, I always think you my friend. I always think that."

"Why, I am, Cora. I am indeed. Are you in some kind of trouble?"

"Yes, suh. I is."

"Well, now maybe we can take care of that! What is it, Cora? Are they after you?"

"It ain't that kind of trouble, Mr. David. It's deeper'n that. It's here." She indicated her generous bosom. "Mr. David, I go to see the picture you have in de theater, almost the first one in. I go in. An' den the picture commence." She paused, so great was her emotion. "It hurt me, Mr. David, to see what you do to my people. I could hardly stan' it. I keep sayin', 'Dis is not my Mr. David. He same name, but he different man.' But I have seen your photo in de paper an' I know it is my Mr. David that I wuk for on East Thirty-seventh Street and we have so many nice talks."

He was genuinely touched. "Why, that's history, Cora. I didn't make it up. My father told me much and I got much out of books."

"It may be history but it not my people. No colored folks ever do like the picture say. Dat place where Mae Marsh run through the forest with Gus after her, an' he ketch up—and she jump off the cliff—that never happen, Mr. David. My people never do dat."

"He was a mulatto, Cora. I am afraid such scenes did take place."

"Finally de picture is over an' I come out, feelin' sick, an' I go in so happy."

"I am sorry, Cora. I am, indeed. I wanted to show how the colored people were misled by white scalawags."

"I don't know what you meant to do—I only know what I see." She paused, choked with emotion. "Mr. David, you see him." She pointed to the little boy. "His name no longer David. It's Thomas."

Griffith was deeply hurt. He again tried to explain his point of view, but Cora saw only hers, and a pained silence rose between them.

Finally she stood up. "Good-by, Mr. David. Come on, Thomas."

Taking the child by the hand, she led him out.

He sat for some moments, a hurt and disturbed man. The telephone rang. Many things to do, many people who wanted to see the man who made the most controversial picture in the history of the world.

Now, for the first time, money was pouring in to him. What would he do with it? What, with money at his command, would the restless, driving man do next?

THE COMPLETE CAST OF
THE BIRTH OF A NATION

Benjamin Cameron	Henry B. Walthall
His sister Florence	Mae Marsh
His sister Margaret	Miriam Cooper
Mrs. Cameron	Josephine Crowell
Dr. Cameron	Spottiswood Aitken
Austin Stoneman	Ralph Lewis
His daughter Elsie	Lillian Gish
His son Phil	Elmer Clifton
His second son	Robert Harron
Silas Lynch	George A. Siegmann
Gus	Walter Long
Lydia Brown	Mary Alden
Abraham Lincoln	Joseph Hennaberry
Charles Sumner	Sam de Grasse
Gen. Lee	Howard Gay
Gen. Grant	Donald Crisp
Jake	Wm. de Vaull
Cyndy	Jennie Lee

CHAPTER 8

HE GOES HOME TO VISIT
HIS MOTHER

THE BUSINESS OFFICE, SEEING ITS POSSIBILITIES, exploited the picture as no other picture had ever been exploited in history. Twelve companies were sent out, each with a print; they moved from town to town, whooping up interest and showing the picture at advanced prices. One of their ways to stir up excitement was to engage men, fit them with robes of the Ku Klux Klan, and have them ride horseback through the streets, ending up at the theater. The Griffith organization called these show-and-exploitation groups "road companies"—and thus, in the show world, the name was born. Printed, circuslike posters were slapped on billboards and thereby marked for the first time in history the use of "twenty-four-sheets" to advertise a motion picture. In many parts of the United States there were no motion-picture theaters. This matter was taken care of by what was called *"Birth of a Nation* Specials." Trains were hired, people were picked up at lonely crossroads, taken to the city, and shown the picture. Usually the people stayed overnight and had a wonderful time. Neighborhoods got together and went by train to the nearest city that had a picture theater and they, also, had a wonderful time. In fact, everybody had a good time, except the harassed Negroes. Schools marched in groups to see the picture, because the picture taught "Americanism."

Every possible angle to exploit the picture was used—all except one. And this was the "personal appearance." No star had yet gone forth to shout for a movie.

The picture brought millions to the box office who never before had gone to a picture house. Until now they had thought of motion pictures in terms of the nickelodeon and the cheap side-street halls where people were requested not to spit on the floor. They came flocking to motion-picture houses, ready to hand over two dollars. It was something new and novel to the American public. The term "the flickers" was completely gone now.

The effect of the players on the public was startling. Until now people had paid little or no attention to the names of the actors—except Little Mary and the Biograph Girl; now the public wanted to know all about the people taking these parts. Nothing like it before had ever been known. Requests for pictures of the players and their autographs poured in; how long it seemed since Little Mary had got twenty-two letters in the ancient days at Biograph.

The public wanted to know about "the Little Colonel"— Henry B. Walthall—and the men of America tried to adopt his fine patrician air; their success was not notable. They imitated his haircut and they wanted his style of collar and necktie. Rough-and-ready men who had once let a lady look after herself as best she could now hopped up and led her across the street as if rescuing her from a burning building. When a man got her across and she thanked him, he took off his hat and laid it reverently across his breast. It was a stirring and ennobling sight.

The effect on the women also was startling. Once plumpness had been queen, but the heroine of *The Birth of a Nation* was slender and petite, and now the women of America wanted to be slender and petite. Their success was not outstanding. Lillian Gish was demure and blushed at a rude word. The women of America tried this, too, thereby startling their men no end. In the picture the heroine was always shaking down her golden, sunlit hair. Our women shook theirs down, too, but not so successfully as the heroine did. Also the heroine was sweet and demure, but when the right man came along she was all fire. The women of America seemed to succeed better here.

Money began to pour in to Epoch Films Corporation. The first thing that Griffith demanded of the business office was to pay off the individuals who had believed in him and had put up their money. The Reverend Thomas Dixon rejoiced in the spotlight that suddenly fell on him. He said that he had believed in the picture from the very first.

Griffith, who had lived in obscurity, was now the most-talked-of man in America outside of political figures. He was criticized and denounced. Now and then a voice piped up and said he had given the world a new art. Such a person, however, was soon put in his place. His attackers said he was killing "the living theater," as they tenderly called it. The Shuberts announced they would hire no one who had had a prominent part in any movie. This didn't quite demoralize the new and growing group called "movie actors." One who came through with calm nerves was Mary Pickford. An item that kept her from trembling too much at the Shubert thunderings was that she was now making $2,000 a week.

D. W. Griffith was thrilled with the overwhelming success of the picture, but secretly looked down on it. It was cheap entertainment for the unthinking masses. He had started out to do something and he had made a success of it. But the thing that he had made a success of was tawdry. The money was coming in; as soon as he had enough of it, he would stop and

do something worth-while. There was that manuscript which
was to establish him as the American Ibsen—*The Treadmill*.
Its great theme would rock the thinking world; the theme that
man was an encumbrance on the earth and that he would
wreck the planet and perish with it.

When interviewers came to see him, he told as little as possible about himself; when he spoke of his early days he said he
was from Louisville, Kentucky, where he had worked on a
paper. Sometimes he told the interviewers he had been an actor,
but spoke of this only briefly. He became sensitive about his
age and gave out that he was born in 1880.

Word came that his mother was not well. She had never
liked Louisville and wanted to go back to the old farm, but
that had been gone many years. But she could return to early
surroundings and her old friends, so he bought a house for her
in LaGrange, six miles from the old homestead and twenty
miles from Louisville.

As soon as he got to Louisville, he was the center of interest.
He had been something of a mystery. After he'd left, little
had been known about him, except that he was actin' in
travelin' shows. Then he'd got "mixed up" in the movies—no
one knew in exactly what way. But now he was back. He was
famous. He was rich.

He walked along the streets where he had pegged so many
times. He went to the house on West Chestnut Street where
the family had lived when they had come from the farm. How
small it seemed. He went to 930 Fifth Street. Why! This was
where he was living when he had been a member of the Meffert Stock Company and had been told that to be a great playwright one must have been an actor. He went to the public
library where he had read Browning and Walt Whitman and

the great storytellers; and he went to the Filson Club with its wonderful library where he had read so long ago.

But really it wasn't so long ago. He had a drive that astonished younger men. His real career was ready to begin. He was making money; he would soon stop making motion pictures. He had an idea for one more picture. That would be the end.

He was touched when he went in to see his mother. She had always been an aristocrat, and, even now, gave off that feeling. She had been Mary Oglesby before she had married his father; yes, a member of the famous and important Oglesby family of Georgia. Here she was now, trembling with excitement to see "her boy." She had lived through Reconstruction; she had told him about it many times. She was proof of what he had shown in the picture.

After the first flurry of greetings the talk went to family history, and she spoke of his grandfather, Daniel Wetherby Griffith, who had been in the War of 1812; and of his father, who had been in the War with Mexico and in the War Between the States.

Her mind was on the past. She asked him if he remembered how he had arrived in Louisville when they had left the farm at Crestwood. He had to study a moment. He had come on a wagon piled high with furniture, bedding, and household effects, he said.

"That's right, David," she said, pleased. "Albert came on the second load." She mused a moment. "I think it was the second load."

How was his health? Was he working too hard?

She paused. "How is Linda?"

"I hear from her now and then—when she wants money."

"Will there have to be a divorce?"

"I don't know. I can't tell yet."

"It's too bad," said his mother sadly. "Do you drink, David?"

"No, Ma."

"I'm glad of that, David. Our men were never drinkers. I often think how your father used to read Shakespeare aloud." She paused; a smile lit up her worn face. "I didn't ever let him know, but sometimes I'd go to sleep."

Griffith laughed. "I expect I did, too."

She peered at him with her dim eyes, now and then blinking. "People send me clippings. I get Mary Bruce to read them to me. They mention the big success your film is. I'm glad of it, David. I'm glad of anything that advances you."

"The picture is doing unbelievably well, Ma. If I have luck I'll make a million dollars this year!"

"I'm pleased things are turning out well. So many times in life they don't." After a moment she seemed to realize how much money that was. "Will you give some to the church?"

"I hadn't thought of that."

"I've always managed to give a little to our foreign missionary work. We used to send the Chinese our old clothes, packed in barrels with camphor balls. I used to smile when I thought how the Chinese, when they opened the barrels, must have got a whiff that was pretty strong!" She again paused; something deep and personal was in her mind. "Naturally I'm glad you have made such a big success of your theater work, but sometimes I wish you had chosen to be a Methodist minister."

"I think I do some good the way it is, Ma. I try to show what is right with the world and what is wrong, at least as I see it."

"I realize you'd want to, David. But things told from a pulpit by a God-fearing man carry a meaning that things in a theater don't have."

"I'm writing a play. I'm very hopeful of it."

"You always ran to theater things, like when you joined the Meffert Stock Company an' acted. I can say it now, but that was a blow. I didn't mind it too much when they took your name off the church books."

They talked of other things, then came back to themselves.

"I do appreciate you buying this house for me, David. It isn't the old family home at Crestwood, but it's cheery and comfortable. I'm willing to stay here until God calls me."

"That'll be a long time yet, Ma." He choked.

She made little clicking sounds, for her teeth did not fit right. "I like to hear you say it, David. God blessed me with good children. Albert writes every week. Mary Bruce brings the mail and reads it to me." There was another pause. "When I go I want to be taken to Mount Tabor and put beside your father and Mattie. I asked Mary Bruce to drive me past it the other day. It looks so peaceful."

At last, deeply stirred, he left. It was the last time he saw her alive. She died December 11, 1915, aged eighty-six. He came back for the funeral and stood beside the grave in the cemetery that had looked so peaceful to his mother.

CHAPTER 9

THE STORY BEHIND THE MAKING
OF INTOLERANCE

THE SUCCESS OF *The Birth of a Nation* GAVE him an opportunity to do something he'd never before had a chance to do. The stories he had been writing had been coming back from the magazines. Well, he would be his own editor and he would accept his own stories. He took the rejected stories, changed them, and made them into films! During the year 1916—with the myriad things he had to do—he made seven films from stories of his own. He put other names on them, but they were all his stories. The list:

1. *The Wood Nymph* written and produced by Griffith; scenario by Granville Warrick. Released January 15. Triangle brand.

2. *Daphne and the Pirates.* Scenario by Granville Warrick.

3. *Hoodoo Anne.* By Granville Warrick.

4. *An Innocent Magdalene.* The original story by Granville Warrick.

5. *The Wild Girl of the Sierras.* Original story by D. W. Griffith.

6. *The Mystery of the Leaping Fish.* Story by our faithful Granville Warrick.

7. *Diane of the Follies.* By Granville Warrick.

Even while he was making *The Birth of a Nation,* he was also working on a picture to follow it, so driven, so restless, so energetic was this amazing man. It was called *The Mother and the Law.* The crux of it was a mother's struggles to get possession of her child who had been taken away from her by a cruel man who owned a mill in the town where the scene of the story was laid. In addition, there was a secondary plot that concerned the woman's young husband who was accused of a crime he had not committed. The poor woman had plenty of troubles, indeed. Just as everybody and everything seemed doomed there was to be a Griffith last-minute run to the rescue, and all was to end with the sun shining and everybody happy. A small story, compared to the mighty *The Birth of a Nation.*

He had assembled a cast and, next morning, rehearsals were to begin and would continue for at least six weeks—backbreaking, temper-shattering rehearsals in which he sometimes coaxed his players in friendly tones, sometimes lashed them with words that were hard to forgive. But, some way or other, the players did forgive him. They all wanted to work for The Master.

In the cast were Mae Marsh, Robert Harron, Miriam Cooper, Monte Blue, Vera Lewis, Ralph Lewis, Douglas Fairbanks, Walter Long, Tod Browning.

Personal Memory: In a letter to the author from Mae Marsh:

The Mother and the Law was the forerunner of *Intolerance;* it became the modern story of that great epoch. One scene called for Robert Harron to be executed, although he was innocent. We did not put the feeling into the scene that Mr. D. W. thought we should, so he took us to San Quentin to see how a condemned man would act before he gave up his life. Motion pictures were made of the prison walls, the yard, the gates, and different places. While we were waiting inside the prison yard, Robert Harron lit a cigarette and started to smoke; just then a prison gate, leading to one section of the yard, opened and half-a-dozen real prisoners started to march by. One of the prisoners passed near Robert Harron. Lowering his voice, the prisoner said, "Buddy, if you drop that cigarette no one will hold it against you."

Robert Harron dropped the cigarette and, later, the prisoner came back and retrieved it.

Miss Margery Wilson played the part of "Brown Eyes," who was the daughter of a Huguenot, in *Intolerance*. "I was," she says, "cruelly murdered." She later became famous as the originator of "the charm school." From her memory book:

One evening at a party at Mae Marsh's house, we placed Mr. D. W. in an easy chair. We would give him a line of poetry, or even a single phrase. In nearly every case he would not only identify the poem but repeat the poem as a whole. His memory was phenomenal.

Once he gave a dinner party. In the center of the table, as a *pièce de résistance*, was a suckling pig on a platter with an apple in its mouth. D. W. was carving and at the same time dissertating on Plato. The apple, jarred by the carving, fell out of the pig's mouth. D. W. picked up the apple, inserted it where it should be, and calmly continued to expound Plato. He had been so absorbed in what he was saying that he had not realized that he had restored the apple to its place.

When I was borrowed by the Thomas H. Ince studio to play opposite William S. Hart, Mr. D. W. sent me in his own limousine. As I was getting into his car, he said, "It would never do for a Griffith leading lady to arrive at another studio on foot."

Rehearsals were always a trying time, for in them the mood of the play must be established. That night Griffith sat alone in his room in the Hotel Alexandria, in Los Angeles, doing what he did every night after the day's end—reading. There came to him with a fresh impact the plight of the little mother in her fight against intolerance and social customs. "Why, it must have been that way since man came upon the earth!" he thought. The idea stirred him; it was true, it was universal, it was important.

There came back to him in a mighty rush of feeling the stories Mattie had read to him as a child. He would trace social injustice through the ages. He would use the little mother in his new story as only part of a mighty story, a story of four periods of time! He would go back to Babylon. He would go to the days of Christ which had meant so much to his own mother. He would go to Paris and tell of the massacre of the Huguenots on Saint Bartholomew's Eve, which Mattie had read to him and which had stirred him so profoundly. And then he would tell the story of the little mother and her fight against injustice. He would, he thought in this moment of exaltation, take these four stories, twenty-four hundred years apart, and weave them together in a film that would stir the world. The idea was breath-taking.

But how to weave them together? He sat for some time, thinking, but getting nowhere. Then he dropped it, as he so often did, and let his subconscious deal with it. By chance he picked up his copy of *Leaves of Grass* and began to thumb through it, flipping the pages, hardly thinking at all what he was doing. Two lines leaped out:

> ... *endlessly rocks the cradle,*
> *Uniter of Here and Hereafter.*

He would have the "little mother" rocking the cradle of life and in the cradle would be the children of destiny.

The cradle would rock between the four stories; it would rock endlessly, just as time goes on without end. People would understand that the cradle was symbolic and that the matter of birth and life held the people of all ages together. He felt ex alted as the sweep and magnitude of the idea laid hold of him, and he began to write excitedly.

In the story would be beauty and pathos and human understanding. He would show Belshazzar, King of Babylon, getting ready to have a feast in the great Hall of Belshazzar, little suspecting that Cyrus, the wicked king of the Persians, was preparing to overthrow him. The feast would be interrupted by the sound of war trumpets and the creaking of the wheels of the mighty war machines. In the second story he would show Julius Caesar and Jesus Christ—war and love—those two mighty drives in human beings. In the third story he would show the King of France with the beautiful ladies of his court. He would make a picture such as had never been made in the history of the world.

He wrote all night.

He could hardly wait to get to the studio to tell Billy Bitzer about it. Billy was there, for he was always the first to arrive: short, stocky, his cap turned backward as usual.

"Billy, I've got something I want to tell you! Y'know, back at Biograph, I once told you we would come to Hollywood and make great pictures and we would become rich?"

"Yah. I remember."

"Well, we're going to make a picture bigger than the *Birth*. It's going to have thirteen reels."

Billy looked up from his tinkering. "T'irteen? Is it you are yoking?"

"We're going to have four stories in one. They run along, each one separate, like little rivers; then they all flow into a mighty river and become one."

"What if dey don't flow?"

"But they will! Part of it is laid in Babylon, twenty-four

hundred years ago. We're going to rebuild the walls of Babylon and they'll be three hundred feet high."

"T'ree hundredt feet high! Who vants high valls? I dun't."

"I do! The world does. And the walls will be so wide on top that a golden chariot with four horses can be driven on it."

It was too much for mystified Billy. "Who wants to drive four horses on a wall t'ree hundredt feet tall? Yah, drive 'em on the ground, but neffer on a vall t'ree hundredt feet."

"And we will show the King of France in his royal court with beautiful girls."

"*Ah!* Now ve get some place."

"And we will have 16,000 extras."

"Andt t'e money, ve vill have it zo?"

"We have the *Birth* money. That's coming in all the time."

"Andt t'e golt chariot . . . ve have money for a golt chariot, yah?"

"I tell you not to worry about the money. I'll take care of that. You'll do the best photography you ever did in your life, won't you, Billy?"

"Yah. It is zo."

Griffith was delighted. He could count on Billy, the greatest motion-picture photographer in the world.

When the cast arrived, he called them together, eager to impart the exciting news. "I've got something to tell you about our story. I've changed it. Our story now is part of a much bigger story, one that has four stories running parallel until they join and end in a smashing climax."

It was all vague to the cast, but The Master could do no wrong.

"I've changed the title. I'm going to call it *Intolerance*, for that is the theme of the story. I had some of that in the way they treated me for *The Birth of a Nation*. I think you'll all be proud to be in it."

And this indeed was true.

The incredible man started with all his amazing energy to make the greatest picture the world had ever seen, a picture that was to dwarf *The Birth of a Nation*, one to be much more important, for it was to deal with all humanity, over all time, and not just with the civil troubles of one nation.

And it all did happen at 4500 Sunset Boulevard, in Los Angeles. The Court of France sprang up and the walls of Babylon sprang up—three hundred feet high and wide enough for Billy Bitzer's "golt chariot." Jerusalem appeared, and so did Julius Caesar. It was all new, it was all unbelievable. But there it was and there were the pop-eyed tourists.

Among the visitors was DeWolf Hopper, the famous actor. Griffith invited him up on the director's lofty platform and there the two, side by side, surveyed the make-believe world below.

"That," said Griffith proudly, "is Jerusalem."

DeWolf Hopper studied the scene, then pointed to a white-robed figure driving a Ford car. "Who is that?"

"That is Jesus Christ entering Jerusalem," said Griffith.

"I think I'll get down now," said DeWolf.

An army of carpenters started work on Belshazzar's banquet hall. Out and out it spread and up and up it went.

At last the whole impossible thing was ready. Cameras were ready to roll, tourists came thicker than ever to see the actors and extras at lunch—peasants carrying lambs on their shoulders, soothsayers, gold-beaters—a vast and colorful crew. There they were—12,000 of them, and among them were Persians, Egyptians, Cyrus' mean and crafty hordes, and a hundred luscious dancing girls. It made the Iowa people gulp.

But extras were not too expensive. They got two dollars a day, plus a sixty-cent lunch.

The cast for the Babylonian story had to be selected; among those he chose were Constance Talmadge, Elmer Clifton, Elmo Lincoln, Mildred Harris, Pauline Stark, Alma Rubens, George Fawcett, and Tully Marshall. One person—not a member of the cast—was a young man named W. S. Van Dyke. He was merely Griffith's helper.

Notable in the cast was a girl named Carol Dempster from Duluth, Minnesota. Her father was a boat captain on the Great Lakes. She had gone to a convent, but now that schooling was over. She made her debut as a dancer in Duluth and had been good enough to join the Ruth St. Denis dancers. She had come to Hollywood and was chosen by Griffith for a dancing part. Much was to come of this decision.

One scene was between The Girl and Belshazzar. At the great feast the girl wrote a love note to Belshazzar. She put the precious missive in a little cart drawn by snow-white pigeons and they took the pulsing letter to Belshazzar, who was three feet away. It taught people a new use for pigeons.

For the story of Christ, he chose, among others, Bessie Love, Lillian Langdon, Olga Grey, Carmel Myers, and Erich von Stroheim to be the wicked Pharisee.

And now the most important player of all—the mother to rock the cradle. He wrote a fancy subtitle to describe Lillian Gish:

A Golden Thread Binds the Four Stories—
A Fairy Girl, with Sunlit Hair—
Her Hand on the Cradle of Humanity—
Eternally Rocking—

The picture started. The vast armies swept over the plains of Mesopotamia; gold chariots raced along the walls; Belshazzar had his feast and died for it; the dancing girls shook their charms. Lillian Gish, with her sunlit hair, rocked eternally.

The cameras ground on day after day. Billy became alarmed.

"Mr. Greeffith, how long it would be?"

"Three hundred reels."

"Is it you yoke?"

"We'll expose that much film, then cut it down."

"Yah. It is goot," said the faithful Billy.

An atmosphere of mystery arose. No one, except the cast, knew what the story was about, and they were not clear, except that people ought to love each other. This they understood, as they fought bitterly to be near the camera.

At last the picture was finished; it had taken fourteen months. The walls and the banquet hall with its elephants still stood. Tourists still came and gaped. The mystery of what it was all about became more profound.

Finally the cameras stopped; it would take seventy hours to run the film. The job of cutting and assembling began. Day after day Griffith sat in the smelly little cutting room, running the negative back and forth, holding it up to his eye, studying it with a magnifying lens, rerunning it. At last it was finished —thirteen reels.

Now came the decisive moment. His financial backers were to see the picture that was to be bigger and better than *The Birth of a Nation*.

They came excitedly and excitedly shook hands with the great director. Over all hung the air of a triumphal opening night. The picture began. The story jumped back and forth over the ages. The cradle rocked on. The money men could not understand it. Was the girl going to have a baby? Was there a surprise in the cradle?

The picture finished in ominous silence.

The puzzled money men looked at one another.

"Is this the final version?" one asked.

"Yes."

"Do you think this is as good as *The Birth of a Nation?*"

"It's a greater work of art."

"The public wants a good picture, not a work of art," said one of the men profoundly.

"I don't understand it," said another.

"It's symbolical," explained Griffith. "It touches all humanity."

"It didn't touch me," said the man cruelly.

A sharp, bitter personal argument arose. Why hadn't he told them about the picture as he'd gone along? Why had he worked in such secrecy? Why did he carry it all in his head? Why did he build such expensive walls? Why did he have so many extras?

His proud, haughty nature was touched. He knew how to make a picture. His judgment shouldn't be questioned. But they questioned it sharply. He'd spent their money and all he had to show for it was thirteen reels of jumbled film.

"You might just as well have reached your hand into our pockets and stolen the money."

"You men haven't faith in this picture, but I have. I will buy it. You can have your money back."

"It'll add up to a million dollars."

"I'll take the picture off your hands at a million dollars."

The men were stunned. Was he just talking? They would find out. "If we have papers drawn up, will you sign them?"

"Gladly," said the haughty man.

He told Billy Bitzer what had happened and what the men had said.

"The men are fools, like always," said the loyal Billy. "It is a goot picture. The valls of Babylon are vonderful, like I said they would be. The shot of t'e gold chariot mit t'e four horses—neffer has dere been one like it against ze sky."

"I appreciate what you say, Billy."

"It vill make mooch money."

"I hope so," said Griffith fervently.

He was silent, for he was not a man to speak easily of anything deep in him. "I'm low in the mouth about the picture. The men not liking it . . . Billy, I've got something to tell you. I bought the picture for a million dollars."

Billy was stunned. "Is it you say a million dollars?"

"Yes. Out of my own pocket."

"Goot. It ees lots of money, but you get lots of picture. Y'know, you once say we come to Hollywood, I andt you, and ve make great pictures togedder. Ve have made it, Mr. Greeffith!"

"I think we have," said Griffith, his spirits rising. "We'll make other great pictures together, won't we, Billy?"

"It is zo," said Billy.

Griffith himself left with a print for New York to get a theater. He seemed hardly to have arrived before the telephone rang. "I guess you know who this is!" said a voice. "May I come up?"

Linda was as good-looking as ever, and did not seem much older. "I saw in the papers you were in town and I knew you would be at the Astor."

He felt ill at ease as he shook hands. Was this all the demonstration, after he had known her so well? Why! It was six years ago they had parted—that day she had announced so proudly that she was going to be leading lady for Kinemacolor.

"I'm glad to see you're not half undressed and swinging those dreadful Indian clubs. Do you still do that?"

"When I have time. My health is good and I attribute some of it to exercise."

After the first greetings he felt nervous, and so did she, but she was much more clever in hiding her feelings.

"I see your new picture has been released. I understand it is thirteen reels."

"Yes. One more than the *Birth*."

"You've come a long way since *The Adventures of Dolly*."

"The whole industry has advanced since then. I've just moved along with it."

"You've moved along at the head of it! In a way, David, you are a genius."

"Thanks, Linda. It's nice of you to say so. I need a little encouragement just now."

"Do you think your new one is going to succeed?"

"I hope so."

"I do, too," she said with an effort at warmth and sympathy. "Was it wise to try to carry four stories at the same time?"

"I thought so when I was working on it."

There was a silence; he sat sprawled out in his chair, the way he so often did his thinking, tapping the ends of his fingers together.

She spoke. "I think you ought—well, to say it bluntly—to send me more money. You've had a big success in *The Birth of a Nation* and you seem to think the new one will catch on."

"I've had to take over *Intolerance* at a million dollars."

"Oh! I think, David, I have as much right to some of that money as those men in Hollywood."

"It's more complicated than that, Linda. Many factors are involved."

"You always want to complicate matters. You did that in the early days. I've talked to my lawyer and I want fifteen per cent of your income."

"I want to be generous with you, Linda, but in this tricky business I may not always have a good income."

"It'll probably get better. You're a genius."

When she left, he had promised to sign the papers.

He was able to engage the Liberty Theatre—where he had had such success with *The Birth of a Nation*—and opened the picture on the night of September 6, 1916.

In Griffith was a strange combination of the maudlin and the bloody; it came out in the silly names he gave his characters, for in this story are to be found Brown Eyes, the Dear One, the Mountain Girl, a Friendless One, Princess Beloved. In contrast to this sentimentality was the scene where Belshazzar's soldiers cut off the head of his enemy. Audiences— lost in the sweetness of the Princess Beloved—shuddered.

The picture was a failure.

He was desperate. He wired his brother Albert L. Griffith to come and take over the management and exploitation of the film. The brother came; he had been in the soap business, but, it was soon found, had a kind of genius for picture work. But the tide was running against the two men.

The picture opened in other cities across the country; it was received with indifference. The picture preached peace; America was drifting into war.

Clune's Auditorium, which had resounded to *The Birth of a Nation*, was cold and unresponsive.

Some cities banned the picture.

Hollywood began to call it "The D. W. Griffith Follies."

He decided to take a print himself to London. England would respond to it. He arrived; the exchange man was delighted to see the great director. Yes, he would arrange to have the picture booked at once.

It opened at the Drury Lane Theatre on the night of April 6, 1917. When Griffith came out, newsboys were standing in front of the theater with their printed banner sheets which said, "United States Declares War on Germany."

CHAPTER 10

HE GOES TO FRANCE TO MAKE A PROPAGANDA PICTURE FOR THE ALLIES

ENGLAND WAS SO DEEP IN THE WAR THAT IT could pay little attention to the picture; on top of this, England, also, could not follow the complicated and involved plot. The critics were kind and said that the picture must live by its picturesque details.

Brother Albert was rushed to Australia where the picture was better received than it had been in the United States or in England.

These were low days for Griffith. His money was tied up in a sick picture. Then, after the way things sometimes happen, a telephone call came in—the Prime Minister wanted to see him! In no time at all he was at 10 Downing Street.

He was delighted to appear before David Lloyd George, but was not awed and ill at ease, for no one ever had greater self-confidence than D. W. Griffith—in spite of *Intolerance*. After all, he'd made *The Birth of a Nation* and was the world's greatest film director.

"I've had one of my staff look you up, Mr. Griffith," said Lloyd George. "May I ask if you're related to Colonel Jacob Wark Griffith of the Confederacy in the American War Between the States?"

"He was my father," said the surprised man.

"I am indeed pleased to meet you. My military aide tells me your father achieved something that has taken a secure place in military history. And that is, he led a cavalry charge from the vantage point of a horse and buggy. Is that true?"

"It is," said Griffith, expanding. "One time he captured fifteen hundred Yankee mules. We're proud of that, too."

The two men, feeling at ease with each other, laughed over this.

"My father," said Griffith more soberly, "was wounded five times and finally died, in later years, chiefly from the effects of his wounds."

"You know quite a bit about war, don't you?"

"I grew up, as a boy, surrounded by war talk, and I have made three pictures with war backgrounds."

"One was *Intolerance*. What were the others?"

"*Judith of Bethulia* and *The Birth of a Nation*."

"Mr. Griffith, would you be willing to help in the war effort?"

"I would, indeed."

"I would like to have you make a war picture. Frankly, it would be propaganda. I would like to have you show the younger people the need for a united effort against our enemies. I will turn over to you our complete resources and I will especially delegate Lord Beaverbrook to help you, and you may know that you have the support of the British Cabinet. If all this is satisfactory, will you want to make a tour of the battlefields?"

"I would like very much to make the tour."

He went from one ruined village to another, talked through an interpreter to the people and asked how they felt when they were being bombed and how it felt when they had to flee from their homes.

What kind of picture should he make? Would it be a spectacular one like *Intolerance* with the armies at each other? Or should it be the story of a girl taken by the enemy and separated from her sweetheart? He pondered the matter. One evening he read in the paper how a French village had been bombed, families separated, children taken from their mothers, girls from their sweethearts. The idea came to him to try to make an audience feel the suffering and loss of having their homes destroyed and their families separated. He would show the suffering and privations of an occupied village. He would let one village and the people in it represent the whole of war. Would the story be big enough? Should a war story be as big as war itself? Should mighty guns roar and legions march?

As he had done when he had gotten the idea for *Intolerance*, he began to write. He wrote all night. By morning the story was laid off into scenes, and was completed. What would he call it? He hit upon *Hearts of the World*. Since it was to be chiefly about a French family, he would give someone else credit, so he wrote:

> Scenario by M. Gaston de Tolignac.
> Translated into English by Captain
> Victor Marier.

As fast as he could manage it, he got to Hollywood. He found Billy Bitzer in the Griffith studio experimenting with lenses and working with chemical baths and tinting fluids. Billy was delighted to see The Master. "How is de picture go in London?"

"We had a bit of bad luck. It opened the day we declared war on Germany."

"Did de paper mention de photography? Anyt'ing about de walls? Maybe de golt chariot, yah? Is eet zo?"

"No, Billy. Not a word."

"Den dey don't know what they see."

"Billy, I've got news for you! We're going to France to make a war picture."

Billy's eyes got big. "Mit lots of cannons? Andt soldiers marching? We take from a platform, is it not?"

"No, Billy. It's going to be a small picture but a big idea."

"What is de big idea?"

"To make the world safe for Democracy."

"Oh!" said Billy disappointedly. "We have dot in *Judith of Betoolia,* but when de war was over, dere was no more Democracy dan before."

"This war is different."

"Who tell you?"

"The Prime Minister of England."

Billy was silent for a moment. "I will do what I can, Mr. Greeffith. Is eet you take de Indian cloobs?"

"Where go I there go my Indian clubs!" said Griffith expansively.

The word got around Hollywood that Griffith was going to make a "war" picture which would be bigger than *Intolerance.*

Meantime, Griffith set to work. Almost the first person he selected for the cast was Adolph Lestina, who had been kind to him in the Meffert Stock Company. He had Lestina in pictures before, he would have him again.

Lillian Gish would play the lead; Dorothy Gish would be a village girl; and now, since their mother was to go along as chaperone, she would be in the cast, too. Robert Harron had been with him at Biograph, and into the cast he went—and his mother, his brother, and two sisters. Others were in the cast—others who had been with him for years: Kate Bruce, George

Fawcett, George A. Siegmann. When he got to England and to France, he would add to the list.

Immediately, when he got to England, he ran into trouble—Billy Bitzer's German background. The secret service put Billy under guard and began to "investigate" him. Griffith explained the situation and the need for haste, but this made no difference to the great secret service. Griffith and the cast were held up three weeks. Finally Billy was cleared and off to France went the company.

Here Griffith added to the cast. A young Britisher came up and said, "I'm an actor and I'd like to get a job."

"The places are all filled, except somebody to play a French peasant who pushes a wheelbarrow."

"I can push a wheelbarrow," said the young man, and he did. His name was Noel Coward.

Griffith also added Erich von Stroheim to play a German army officer. Even here, within sound of the guns, he rehearsed the players as of old.

So much attention had the making of the film attracted that he was invited to meet Queen Alexandra, consort Queen of King Edward the Seventh—quite a way up for a boy who had once run a rope elevator.

Back to Hollywood, where many of the interior scenes were made. The picture must be cut, and soon he was again in the evil-smelling little room, running the negative back and forth and peering at it with his enlarging lens.

Hollywood waited eagerly to see the "war" picture that was to be greater than *Intolerance*. He took it to Clune's Auditorium where *The Birth of a Nation* had opened three years and one week ago. But no hooded horsemen clattered through the streets; no Negroes stood pressed against the wall.

Again, as was so often the case with Griffith, he had over-sentimental subtitles. One was, "Month after month piled up its legend of Hunnish crime on the Book of God."

The audience was disappointed. Why! it wasn't a big picture at all—not a Griffith super. No towering walls. No Nubian lions. It was a small picture, dealing only with a village and its people. But it was moving; it showed what war did to people. One believed in the characters and one suffered with them.

Griffith himself took a print and rushed to New York, as he had done with *Intolerance*. It opened at the Forty-fourth Street Theatre, April 5, 1918. The audience reaction was about the same as it had been in Los Angeles—good, but not the work of a master. No Pinkerton detectives. No call by the mayor. Was he slipping? Had he seen the heights and was he going down the slopes? Would the exhibitors want to book his next picture?

He was forty-three.

He kept up his Indian-club swinging; to this he added sparring with a boxing partner. He engaged Kid McCoy and nearly every evening the two went to the gymnasium, and thus Griffith got a new kind of exercise. He was immensely proud of his athletic ability and said that if a ruffian ever attacked him on the streets he would be able to take care of him.

He still owed on *Intolerance*. He had to have money and, with his amazing drive, he started in to make "commercial" pictures, filming three in rapid succession: *The Great Love, The Greatest Thing in Life, A Romance of Happy Valley*.

In the first he used the players that had been with him so long and so successfully: Lillian Gish, Henry B. Walthall, Robert Harron, George Fawcett, Rosemary Theby, Carol Dempster, George A. Siegmann.

In the second he had his great favorite Lillian Gish, Robert

Harron, Elmo Lincoln, Kate Bruce, David Butler, and his long-time friend Adolph Lestina.

And these same players, with a few changes, were the ones who appeared in *A Romance of Happy Valley*.

Hollywood was puzzled. Here was Griffith, who had made so many war pictures and pictures dealing with war, now making pictures about a boy and a girl having a hard time getting married! Could this be The Master? Why! there were half-a-dozen directors who could have made these run-of-the-mill pictures.

Ambitious new directors were coming into pictures—directors who were using the effects that Griffith had invented, men who hardly knew he had invented them—and cared less.

He eyed these men who had the drive he'd had when he had first started. They would never catch up, he thought.

He had grown more and more important, and had come to represent the motion-picture industry. Hollywood and its way of life was beginning to attract public attention; in fact, so much attention did it attract that Frederic and Fanny Hatton wrote a play dealing with Hollywood and its madness. It was entitled *The Squab Farm*. A squab, as set forth by the authors, was a young and innocent girl—a chicken, as later the poor unfortunate was called. The "farm" was the movie studio where the squabs were prepared for public approval.

D. W. Griffith, the renowned director, was the hero of the play; the part was played by Lowell Sherman. The play opened at the Bijou Theatre, New York, March 13, 1918. Griffith came in and seated himself; all watched him. How would he take this thinly disguised portrait of himself? Would there be a lawsuit? This proud southerner.

The curtain went up. Griffith sat with an iron face. And then the digs about Hollywood and motion pictures began. As they popped over the footlights, he was delighted and began to laugh in his heavy, far-carrying voice. Every time a shaft was fired into Hollywood, he applauded.

The plot dealt with the make-believe Griffith and his difficulties in teaching would-be starlets how to act. One of the girls was to play Eve and was to play it adorned as Eve had been in the Garden of Eden. But the noble girl wouldn't emulate her great ancestor, and caused the harassed director no end of trouble. The thin plot was merely a chance to throw barbs into Hollywood.

The star was Alma Tell. The New York critics praised her. Not one wrote a word about a girl who was a member of the cast—Tallulah Bankhead.

This is what she wrote about the matter in her autobiography *Tallulah:*

I got my toe in the theater, thanks to a letter from Daddy to a nabob in the Shubert office. J. C. Huffman needed four young girls—walk-ons—to dress up the stage in *The Squab Farm*. I applied and was named one of the squabs. The play was an attempt to satirize the lunacies of Hollywood.

Although programmed, only one critic noticed us—the *New York World* man. This is what he said: "There are four girls in the company who might better be back in the care of their mothers."

I was too jumpy to have any idea of the merit, or lack of merit, of the play. The rehearsals were a nightmare. The other girls had had experience. The four of us dressed together. When I whistled in the dressing-room, they wanted to lynch me. I was horribly hurt and cried my heart out. Julie Bruns, one of the featured players, took pity on me and let me share her dressing-room. This further alienated the other girls. I was so hell-bent on looking sophisticated that I made up like Theda Bara.

The show played three days in New Haven, then got ready to open in New York. On the day it was to open, one of the papers ran a story based on my grandfather, my father and Uncle John. The catchline said, "Society Girl Goes on the Stage." This libel said I had the featured role. Though none of my doing, the story irked the other members of the company, particularly Alma Tell. Immediately I was aware they thought me guilty of the unpardonable sin—seeking billing beyond deserts. Now what should happen? My Aunt Louise bounced into town two days before the opening. Terrified, I approached one of the girls who had a single line and pleaded with her not to speak that line on the night Aunt Louise would be in the audience. Graciously she consented. When my cue came, I was so shriveled with fear I couldn't open my mouth. A nasty little stage wait ensued. The girl who had befriended me was bawled out by the stage manager who thought she had dried up. The play lasted only four weeks, which was fortunate, for I was Typhoid Mary.

Griffith's dislike of Hollywood and motion pictures took form in other ways. One was for what he called the "silly" names the girls were taking. He spoke of this often and always belittlingly. Among the pretentious names were Arline Pretty, Elinor Fair, Billy Dove, Bessie Love, Louise Lovely, Blanche Sweet—the latter one of his stars.

He still did not have enough money; none of the men who had backed *Intolerance* must lose a penny. His high sense of honor drove him on. He made *The Girl Who Stayed at Home*. It would have been better if Griffith had stayed at home. And he made *True Heart Susie*, who may have had a true heart but little more. The simple girl fell in love and sold her cows so the boy could go to college and get an education. What happened was shocking. The ungrateful wretch fell in love with another girl. But at last her good heart won him from his foolishness. The film opened at the Strand Theatre, New York, March 23, 1919. The critic for the New York *Evening Mail* said it was endearing, and would be as enduring as Dickens' Christmas Carol. "It's the kind of story," he wrote, "that makes you both laugh and cry at the same time." It seemed that he was alone in his tears, for the other critics said that Susie, in spite of her noble heart, was close to being a downright bore.

Mary Pickford was making $1,000 a day for every day of the year. Griffith was struggling along with commercial pictures and the immense debt he had agreed to pay for the making of *Intolerance*.

Griffith was proud of the way Little Mary had succeeded. He had discovered her; he had, in a way, made her. The appeal she had to a world audience was almost unbelievable; at the age of twenty-three she was the most valuable property in motion pictures. She represented Goodness lined up against Badness. No one in any audience had any doubt which side would win, but the people sat breathlessly watching. She was retelling the old "rags to riches" story, but she had a dozen golden curls and lovely eyes to do it with. She was so innocent and big-eyed that every male in the audience wanted to rush to her side and send the villain about his business; the men didn't seem to know that if they would be patient she would take care of the matter herself. She showed that if you thought good thoughts and had Faith, then everything would turn out right. Life—her pictures preached—was what you made it. The world public thought this was true and started in to remake their lives. The result was exhilarating—especially at the box office.

Griffith, astute showman that he was, knew all this. It did not agree with his view of life, but he was delighted that Mary Pickford was giving the world what it wanted and getting well paid for it.

Meantime for him the nights were long and they were restless. What should he do next? What kind of picture? He must not let his health run down, and so he kept up his Indian-club swinging and his sparring with Kid McCoy.

CHAPTER 11

HE HAS A TREMENDOUS SUCCESS
IN BROKEN BLOSSOMS

FROM THE VERY BEGINNING HE HAD DEALT IN sweet and noble girls—girls who had never had an unworthy thought in all their pure lives. Mary Pickford was a good example. He had a little twist for making her delectable. This was to have her photographed, in the early part of a film, holding a white rabbit. And often he dressed Mary in white, representing purity. This was not pointed up, but there it was psychologically. If another kind of woman had to be in the story, she was shown as much older and as a town gossip. No director could get as much out of a town gossip as D. W. Griffith could. Often he used two, so they could react on each other.

Suddenly there swept across the screen a female vastly different from Griffith's noble girls. She appeared first in *A Fool There Was;* she was not only ignoble but as dangerous as an adder. The foul creature would come at night, or when the victim was unprepared, and suck its blood and let the victim die a horrible death.

"Vampire" was shortened into "vamp," and suddenly America became "vamp" conscious. Every high school had a vampire or two going about their horrible business. Boys, who should have known better, were fascinated by them.

A Cincinnati girl was the one who started the whole shocking business. Her name was Theodosia Goodman, the daughter of a tailor. She was in the film version of the stage play *A Fool There Was*. She was supposed to play a character known as "Arab Death," but this was too horrible to pass on to sensitive audiences, so a thoughtful publicity department renamed her Theda Bara. Bara was Arab spelled backward and the word Death was moved a little off center so that it became Theda. The publicity department said she was the daughter of a French soldier and a native Egyptian girl and that she was born in Egypt. At a press conference she was asked where exactly in Egypt she was born.

"On the banks of the Nile," she said.

She was reminded that the Nile was two thousand miles long and was asked where on the Nile.

"On the left bank," she said.

She was frightfully evil. Men sold their souls for a smile. Old men especially sold out; when she had drained them of the last drop of their financial blood, she would light a cigarette and look around for another fool.

Griffith thoroughly disliked the idea of such a woman. He still believed in white rabbits, but white rabbits were losing out. He was shocked that the public no longer wanted the kind of girl he had built his reputation on. But the crowd were going to the theaters where the vampire was showing, not to the one with the white rabbits. He was embittered, but consoled himself by saying this was typical of motion pictures, that pandered only to the lowest.

Would the craze for the dangerous woman pass, and once more the sweet and innocent girl come back into public liking?

However, now and then he had taken excursions into the macabre. There was Judith who danced so shockingly with

Holofernes' head. But this was only a passing interest for him. He had built his reputation on something else, indeed.

Other matters were happening. In February 1919 the Four Greats met in an office in Hollywood: Mary Pickford, Douglas Fairbanks, Charlie Chaplin, and D. W. Griffith. As Griffith sat in one of the big leather chairs that business offices believed they had to have, he looked at Mary Pickford. Was it possible that ten years had passed since she had come that day to the old Biograph studio? She still had the same golden curls, the same winsome ways, the same appealing manner.

"Mary, do you remember in *Pippa Passes* how you carried a guitar and pretended you were playing and singing?"

"I do. And I remember how you wanted to pay me only five dollars for a day's work!"

"And I remember how you made me shake loose of ten dollars! Mr. McCutcheon denounced me bitterly."

They laughed almost tearfully over what they called "the old days."

"Do you remember how you bit me?"

"I do, and I remember you deserved it. I remember how you called Lottie and me 'wild cats.' If that doesn't deserve a bite, I don't know what does. Also I remember how you followed me to the sidewalk and begged me to come back to the set."

"I remember that, too," Griffith said.

"If I hadn't gone back . . . I might not be in pictures today."

The two thought about the wonder of life, the almost overwhelming effect of a small incident.

"And I remember how my dress was pinned up in the back so I couldn't turn my back to the camera."

They laughed about this.

"Oh!" said Mary banteringly. "How did you ever come out in that terrific fight you had with that stuffed eagle?"

Even now he was ashamed of how he had started in pictures.

"I remember, Mr. Griffith," continued Mary, "when you invented the close-up, how the audiences stormed and stomped because the actors on the screen were shown without legs!"

"I certainly remember it," said Griffith wryly. "I was almost fired for cutting off their legs."

"Do you remember the day Lionel Barrymore came down to the studio, ashamed to be seen on the premises?" she asked.

"I do," declared Griffith. "But he wasn't the only one. Some were using assumed names."

He looked at Douglas Fairbanks and spoke with a pretense at severity. "And don't forget, young man, I was the one who gave you your start in pictures. It was in *The Lamb* and you were not any too good."

"You asked me to play in your next picture," said Fairbanks.

"Lay it to my kind heart," said Griffith.

The businessmen came, and personal talk had to be dropped.

When the meeting was over, the United Artists had been organized. It had the greatest stars in the world, and the greatest director. It would do wonderful things.

He delayed, uncertain what to do. He must, as one of the Four Greats, make an important picture. But that was easier said than done.

Mary Pickford came to him aglow with excitement. "Mr. Griffith, I've been reading a book called *Limehouse Nights,* by Thomas Burke. Limehouse is in London and the story has a London background. There's a chapter in it that might make a movie."

"What is it?"

"The chapter is called 'The Chink and the Child.' It has

to do with a British girl who falls in love with a Chinese but is opposed by her brutal father. It's beautiful and touching."

Griffith read the chapter and was so stirred that he began, then and there, to make an outline. And he did as he had done so many times before—wrote all night. In the morning, as he was swinging his Indian clubs, the title came to him: *Broken Blossoms. The White Girl and the Yellow Man.* Later he shortened this to the first two words.

First was to get his favorite, and this he did—Lillian Gish. And soon he had the complete cast:

The Girl	Lillian Gish
The Chinaman	Richard Barthelmess
"Battling Burrows," the Girl's Father . . .	Donald Crisp
His Manager	Arthur Howard
Evil Eye	Edward Peil
A Prize Fighter	Kid McCoy
The Spying One	George Beranger

The latter was the company manager and was to appear only as a brief bit, hardly a player at all.

The gossip got out that Griffith was making a "Chinese picture." That would be absurd, said wise and knowing Hollywood. Nobody wanted to see a Chinese love story laid in the slums of London. He was going to miss it again.

The plot was simple: the girl was in love with a Chinese and was determined to marry him. The father, a coarse creature, was determined there would be no marriage. In the end, the father killed the girl to keep her from marrying the Chinese.

The plot, told in this way, was bald and shocking. But it

did not have the direction of the inspired Griffith, nor his vision of what he could do with his players. In scene after scene The Master rose to heights he had never before attained: the girl cringing before her father's whip, the ruffians dragging her along the banks of the river as seen through a fog.

The attention he gave to details was astonishing. There was to be a musical accompaniment, and when the girl died he wanted to get music that would suggest her death struggle and the flight of her soul to the rich beyond. He worked for two days, going over and over the cue music in this scene which would last six seconds, but was not satisfied; nothing like the release of a soul. Billy Bitzer suggested a Russian orchestra; the orchestra was brought to the studio. Finally Griffith hit on the idea of using a balalaika instrument; he tried one, liked it, and finally used four to give the effect he wished. In his care for detail he was tireless; and he was tireless, too. Every night, before he went to bed, he either read or worked on one of his secret plays.

Then came the days in the cutting room with Jimmie Smith, his cutter; the endless running of the negative back and forth, the peering at it through the enlarging lens. At last it was done. Would the simple story appeal to an audience fed on violence?

When the picture was assembled, he showed it to Adolph Zukor, his principal backer. Zukor watched it in icy silence, relieved now and then with a resentful squirm. When it was over, he said, "It's not a good program picture. We can't sell it successfully."

The George M. Cohan Theatre was engaged. Many leaders of New York were to be there: Sir Thomas Lipton, William Gibbs McAdoo, Charles Dana Gibson, Douglas L. Elliman, Nathan Straus, Dr. Christian F. Reisner, Rabbi Joseph Silverman, Rupert Hughes, Frank Crowninshield, Ben Ali Haggin. In the audience were Lillian Gish and Richard Barthelmess.

The picture opened the evening of May 12, 1919. Special seats were three dollars each—the highest price ever charged for a motion picture.

It was a tremendous success. Critics called it "the perfect picture."

The Master had come back.

The success of the picture was phenomenal. For some time the trade papers had been calling him "the Belasco of the screen"; now he became "the Shakespeare of motion pictures" —quite an elevation for a man who had started his career fighting an eagle.

His ambitions soared. He was going to build a theater of his own to be called "The Griffith." Not only that but he was going to build a chain of theaters across the country to show only his pictures.

With his success he became more arrogant than ever. "They thought they had me down, but they didn't. Let the young directors come along. I know things they'll never know."

He paid on the indebtedness of *Intolerance*.

CHAPTER 12

HE HAS ANOTHER SUCCESS
IN WAY DOWN EAST

As THE FOUR GREATS BEGAN TO WORK TO-
gether, Griffith could not understand the elfin Charlie Chaplin.
Griffith had little taste for comedy, especially the alley comedy
of "The Little Man," as he called him. Chaplin, on the other
hand, had little enthusiasm for the cold and aloof director who
went in so heavily for war and dewy-eyed girls. Nor could
Griffith understand Douglas Fairbanks. "Fairbanks thinks that
acting is leaping from one place to another," he said scornfully.

Mary Pickford was the peacemaker and, some way or other,
managed to keep the men—so completely different—from flying at each other.

Griffith began to develop certain principles in the making
of stories. One was, "It's better to appeal to the heart than to
the head. After all, the theater is a place of dreams." His men
might be remarkably strong and his women wondrously pure,
but that was the way the public wanted them, and a showman's
first duty was to please his customers. Nevertheless, he still
looked down on motion pictures as shoddy entertainment. In
the plays he was secretly writing his men would be more
nearly human and his women less rosebud lipped.

It pained him to see some pictures on the screen—such
films as *The Perils of Pauline;* Tom Mix, the "cowboy" born

in a Pennsylvania coal-mining town; the so-called "vampires," the desert sheiks, the cross-eyed comedian that Mack Sennett found so delightful; obese men like Fatty Arbuckle. How could the public stomach them, when he couldn't get his plays produced?

Again what story to make was the problem. Half the success was the choice of story. If the story was weak, then no matter how skilled the direction, the photography, and the editing, the production would have little appeal. And he must keep money coming in, to be paid to the backers of *Intolerance*, for he had an almost fanatic determination to pay off that indebtedness. In addition, there were the payments to Linda.

He made two hasty productions: *Scarlet Days* and *The Greatest Question*, both weak sisters. On top of this he moved his studio from Hollywood to Mamaroneck, New York, in a mansion built by Henry M. Flagler. He would do great things here. He would do another *Broken Blossoms*.

Did he want to make a great spectacle, or a boy and girl walking hand in hand into the sunset?

In addition there was the sense of rivalry he felt toward the other three. He must make as good a picture as any of theirs. These three had all made pictures that were becoming more and more popular. Mary Pickford was getting a million dollars a year. The Jumping Jack was rising as a box-office star. And The Little Man was gaining a world-wide audience. Why did a pair of baggy pants and a cane have such an appeal?

One day, when Griffith was holding up his nose, the business manager for United Artists said: "D. W., did you know that the Fairbanks pictures and the Chaplin pictures are making more money than yours?" Griffith had known it, in a way, but here it was baldly stated by somebody who knew. They were devastating words. How, he asked himself, could silly comedies and wall-jumping pictures outsell fine stories of real people? Well, his next picture would be an unusually good one.

Brother Albert suggested the stage play *Way Down East,* a crossroads story in which all had noble hearts, except the villains, whose hearts were as stovelids. Griffith didn't know whether he wanted to do such a bucolic story or not, but when he looked into it he found that the play had a remarkable history. Lottie Blair Parker, from Otsego, New York, had gone to Boston to a school of expression to learn to give "dramatic readings," just then a popular form of torture. She studied this device for a while, then drifted into acting and soon was playing in support of Dion Boucicault; then she had written this play of noble hearts and downright meanness. It had first been produced in 1898 and had been going great guns ever since. After it had been running a short time, William A. Brady cast his eye upon it and all he saw was beauty. And so he bought the play from the author, and owned it fore and aft.

Brother Albert went seeking information. "How much do you want for it, Mr. Brady?"

"One hundred and seventy-five thousand dollars."

Brother Albert was a bit stunned and so was D. W.

D. W. entered into a series of protests with Brady which got nowhere impressively. And so the money was paid over. None of it went to the author, which would seem to show how things were in 1920. Anthony Paul Kelly was paid three thousand dollars to adapt it to the screen; now, for the first time, Griffith had a scenario.

When the businessmen heard that Griffith had paid that much for just the *story*, they knew where he would end.

The story dealt with the fine people of New England, with

a few mean characters thrown in just to be true to New England. The snow scenes were made in Central Park, New York, and then the cast was taken to New London, Connecticut, to wait for the ice in the Connecticut River to break. The ice stubbornly refused to break.

Griffith took care of this by going to an open part of the river and having the carpenters saw boards, make platforms and paint them. Then he made the picture. The audiences were thrilled to see the good people in the story escape over the treacherous ice just in the nick of time. No dogs.

Finally the picture was finished. It had cost $1,004,662.

The picture opened in New York in August 1920.

It was a huge success.

People said that the ice scenes were thrillingly realistic.

Again The Master had succeeded. He would always succeed, his followers said. He would always be The Master. No man, as great as he was, could be pulled down, especially when he had such a star as Lillian Gish. Then in June of that year there was the startling news that Lillian Gish had left him to join another company.

In spite of his supporters, detractors were springing up. One detractor said bitterly, "The man sees love in terms of a cooing dove and death in the terms of a falling rose petal. We need something stronger than these pallid depictions."

Griffith needed even more money coming in; so he did as he had done twice before after outstanding successes—turned out a potboiler. In fact, this time he turned out two. One was *The Love Flower*, the other was *Dream Street*, neither of which sent adjectives flying. His touch was as sure as ever.

However, he was forty-six. New, vigorous directors were coming into the field. But this didn't alarm this man who had such supreme self-confidence. After all, he'd made *The Birth of a Nation* and *Broken Blossoms*.

He remembered the French play *The Two Orphans* which had been playing off and on in America for forty-eight years. Great names had adorned it like stars on a Christmas tree. It had been written originally by Adolph d'Ennery and Eugène Cormon and had been translated into English by half-a-dozen different people. The story embraced some of the great historical names in France: Danton, Robespierre, King Louis XVI.

Griffith went to see Lillian Gish. "I want you to come back with me," he said. She was touched; after all, he had made her and, for that matter, she had made him. Together they could not be defeated. That was what he believed and it was what she believed.

Lillian agreed to come back.

The moment he found he could star both Lillian and Dorothy Gish, his mind was made up. He adapted the story to suit his two stars, and he changed the title to *Orphans of the Storm*. The story:

The parents of the two girls had died of the plague; the sisters were being sent to Paris where relatives would take care of them. Dorothy, who was blind, had to be led by her sister. And so into the Paris-bound coach the two girls got, never dreaming of the trouble they were also getting into. The coach was rolling nicely along when out from his vast estate came the great and powerful Marquis de Praille in his Normandy coach, with mounted outriders and coachmen attired in elegant uniforms. It so happened that the girls' coach came along at exactly the wrong moment and blocked the marquis' coach, whereupon the marquis flew into a rage and began to beat the boys attending the girls' coach. As he was whacking away, his eyes fell on Lillian's frightened face. He stopped his wicked blows, adjusted his silk shawl and his lace muff, and approached Lillian, who was too frightened to speak. He found where she was going in Paris and a low plan entered his unworthy head. Finally his coach rolled on, and Lillian breathed a sigh of relief, not knowing what the dastardly man was up to.

He waited until she was safely at her destination, then sent his servant to abduct her and bring her to a grand fete he was giving in his town gardens. In spite of all she could do, the evil man took her there, and stood menacingly in the background to see that she did not escape. Dorothy, poor girl, had been left behind. She, too, had her share of trouble, for she fell into the hands of Madame Frochard, who had not a spark of goodness in her twisted soul.

When things looked blackest for Lillian, two men fell in love with her. The men were mixed up in the political situation and pretty soon were fighting over her like tigers. One was the noble Danton and the other a villain if there ever was one— Robespierre. Danton represented the common people, Robespierre the long-haired boys. Things got so bad that Robespierre demanded Lillian's life and she was led to the guillotine. She was saved in the nick of time by the noble Chevalier de Vaudrey who, as the play ended, took her off to a little vine-covered cottage by the sea. Lillian said that her poor, unfortunate sister should go with her, but at the right moment another noble man showed up, took Dorothy by the hand, and the story ended in moonlight and roses.

To the critical, the plot might seem absurd and silly, but with the glamour that Griffith was able to surround it with, it set audiences by the ears. They lived and suffered with the two girls and rejoiced when Lillian nailed the right man down.

Cast of the principals:

Henriette	Lillian Gish
The Blind Sister	Dorothy Gish
The Mean Marquis	Morgan Wallace
Chevalier de Vaudrey . . .	Joseph Schildkraut
Louis XVI, King of France	Leo Kolmeri
Madame Frochard	Lucille La Verne
Danton	Monte Blue
Robespierre	Sidney Herbert
Sister Genevieve	Kate Bruce
Picard	Creighton Hale
The Doctor	Adolph Lestina

The last was Griffith's good friend from the early days.

Griffith prepared to give his genius for authenticity and detail. The room in the palace where the king was to appear was a replica in the dimension, decorations, and paintings of the grand salon in the Palace of the Kings, in Versailles.

With the complete confidence in himself he'd had when he made *The Birth of a Nation,* he thought only of the story and not the money.

The picture moved along.

At last he entered the evil-smelling room with Jimmie Smith, and there began the running back and forth of the negative. The work was done, the prints were made.

The biggest electric announcements that had ever been seen on Broadway lifted their heads and told the world about the wonders that soon could be seen at the Strand Theatre.

And there it opened May 7, 1922.

It was another fabulous success.

The Master had scored again. He would always score.

The usually reserved New York *Sun* said: "One has to look away to keep from being swept away by the flood of events." The other New York papers let the people look after themselves in the flood of events.

Griffith was delighted, but was secretly discontented. He had, he thought, only ground out another sausage. As soon as he had his debts paid off, he would drop the whole miserable business of picture making and do something worth-while.

He was the most popular, the most-sought-after man on Broadway; everybody wanted to meet this "genius of the films." Interviewers came. He told little about himself. Mostly he said he was from Louisville, Kentucky; sometimes he said he was from LaGrange. He said that he was born in 1880 and that he had been a newspaperman in Louisville. He did not mention that he had had a play produced in Washington. That was too long ago. He gave the impression, without quite saying so, that his only interest was in making motion pictures.

Now and then he would get a letter from Linda; sometimes she called by long distance. "I need a little more money, D. W.," she would say in her overly sweet voice. "I'm not doing so well in pictures."

"How much, Linda?"

She would tell him; there would be an expression of good wishes, and the conversation would be over.

To those he knew and to the people he met he never mentioned her. In fact, many did not know he had ever been married.

He continued to live a double life—the one the public saw, the one no one saw. He lived in the Hotel Astor. Once, when he was asked why he liked the hotel so much, he said, "When

I first came to New York, I used to look at it in awe. The great and powerful lived there—that's why I like to live there."

He liked to go to the theater, where he sat absorbed in the scenes before him. Sometimes he went to a motion-picture theater where he sat coldly and silently watching the film run by; sometimes, in the middle of the picture, he would get up and stalk out.

He enjoyed associating with actors. He was a member of The Players, where he treated even the small fry with great respect; they were playing on Broadway, something he had never been able to do. For statesmen and the international great he had no fear at all. But in the presence of the great actors he was meek and sometimes talked not at all, but kept his grayish-blue eyes fastened on them, laughing when they laughed, growing serious when the conversation turned that way.

He liked to go to Times Square before theater time and watch to see if he could spot any actors hurrying to the theater. There the tall, thin, spare, big-nosed man would stand, eagerly watching.

One evening he saw Lionel and John Barrymore walking arm in arm. A little of the awe he had for great actors came over him; however, he threw this off and stepped boldly forward.

"Hello, Lionel! How are you?"

Lionel looked at him impersonally. "Oh, yes, Griffith! This is my brother Jack."

John Barrymore grunted, then let his eyes wander off into the crowds.

Griffith spoke eagerly. "Do you remember, Lionel, how you came down to the old Biograph on East Fourteenth Street?"

"Yes, I remember it. Long time ago, wasn't it? I believe I was in a picture you directed, wasn't I?"

"Yes. *The New York Hat.* You were what we called an 'uptown actor.'"

"Yes, I do remember they were called that. Well, we'll have to hurry along."

In a moment the two were gone. Griffith stood looking after them.

CHAPTER 13

HE STARTS DOWNHILL

ONE DAY HIS BUSINESS MANAGER TOLD HIM exceedingly good news and in no time he was on the train. He had made many trips to Hollywood; this was to be the most satisfactory.

Los Angeles had changed since he had arrived for the first time and set up a studio. Central Park, where the Clansmen had ridden to herald *The Birth of a Nation*, was now Pershing Square. An office building stood where his actors had once braved the cameras.

He went out to see where *Intolerance* had been made—that was seven years ago. Here it was that the Pacific Electric Railway System of southern California had laid a track to the entrance of Babylon to carry extras and food supplies and to transport the elephants and Nubian lions. The track was gone, but as he walked here and there a sight-seeing bus came roaring up with a man with a megaphone shouting out Griffith's name and telling of the wonders of the great hall where the Feast of Belshazzar had been held.

Jerusalem had been torn down and the City of Paris, as it had been on St. Bartholomew's Eve, was in the grip of a real-estate "subdivider"—a cruel fate. He looked about him sadly. Was his life's work over? Or would he go still higher? What an inscrutable creature Fate was! Why, he was forty-seven! He had not accomplished nearly so much as he had hoped when he had been a young man in Kentucky. He had thought of himself then as a genius. . . .

He walked along the great walls. Plaster elephants still stood on their hind legs, their forelegs in front of them, their trunks uplifted. Bird-beaked deities looked down with a single eye on the inconsequential humans; they themselves lived with the gods.

Pausing, he looked about him uncertainly. It must have been here that the great siege towers had stood—mighty affairs that held fifty warriors, the towers pushed forward by slaves on the ground. Here he had sent up a balloon, with a basket underneath, and in it had been Billy and himself; and here he had leaned over the side of the basket and with his megaphone had shouted orders to the extras below. Oh! those were glorious days. Don't we ever know, until it is too late, when we are in our glorious days? What a great, what a touching concept he'd had for his drama. How poorly the public had responded. But that was the way of mass entertainment. If he had put this concept into a stage play, the result would have been different. He'd get back to his playwriting. He'd do some serious creative work.

Finally he left, touched by what he had seen and felt. He came later to the business office—the same office, it seemed, with its garish decorations and its great unwieldy leather chairs. How many times he had sat with businessmen he couldn't understand, and who couldn't understand him—the eternal conflict between business and art.

There was talk; there were jokes—of a sort.

At last the big, the exciting, the wonderful moment had come.

"Gentlemen," said Griffith, "I am prepared to pay off the

rest of the indebtedness on *Intolerance*. Not one investor has lost a penny."

It had taken seven years, but he had accomplished it.

The men were pleased. It was nice of him to take his responsibility so seriously.

He went to see Mack Sennett, who was big and hearty and glad to see his old friend. Mack spoke of *The Curtain Pole* with which he had knocked 'em around so humorously. What was Wally doin' now? Good gracious, how quickly you got out of touch with people who once had been so important to you!

My! how much time had passed since the "early days." Mary Pickford had divorced Owen Moore and was now married to Douglas Fairbanks and was living in fabulous "Pickfair."

Mack asked cautiously after Griffith's new picture.

It was going to be great, Griffith said. It had a message.

Mack rubbed his chin and chewed his tobacco.

"What you want a message for, D. W.?"

"I like to say something worth-while," said Griffith, a bit sensitive, now that he had been challenged.

"The public isn't interested in messages. They want to laugh."

"What," asked Griffith, "is the basis of comedy?"

The mighty Mack took another chew. "If it seems funny to me, it's comedy."

Griffith was puzzled. The answer made sense. After all, didn't he himself make pictures to suit himself? Wasn't Mack doing the same? Was a director at his best when he made pictures for himself? But, he had to admit to himself, the business office was having more and more to say about the kind of pictures he made.

"What are your stories usually about?" Griffith asked.

"I find the plots of my stories either in crime or sex. You're on safe grounds there."

At last Griffith had to go. The two men, so utterly dissimilar, shook hands heartily. Each had respect for the other, but not understanding.

Griffith went back to New York, happier and more content than he had been in years. He didn't owe a cent, except the money he had to pay Linda—15 per cent of all he made.

He would do a few more pictures, then he would have enough money put by to do something worth-while. But he didn't put it by; he became one of the big spenders on Broadway. Down-and-out actors came with outstretched hands. He'd been one once himself. Hadn't he picked hops in California? And worked in a steel mill in Tonawanda, New York? And with a pick and shovel in the subway in New York? And, when a show had closed, hadn't he hoboed his way from Minneapolis to Louisville?

Such incredible energy had he that he was able to work at night. In his bathrobe he would write into the morning. He sent stories out; they came back. He worked on his plays. *The Treadmill* was giving him trouble. But he would solve it, he told himself. Great plays were not written at a sitting. Strangely enough, he did not show his plays to any of the actors who came to him applying for work. He would write the play alone and by himself. The play was getting better all the time.

One evening the telephone rang. A voice said, "Is dot Mr. Greeffith?'

"Where are you, Billy?" said Griffith, delighted.

"Down in der lobby."

"Come a-runnin', Billy."

This was strange, Griffith thought as he put away his writing things. In all the years he'd known Billy, Billy had never come to the hotel and he himself had never been to Billy's home.

There he was in a few moments—thick of chest, square of shoulder—that great genius of the camera. On his head, this time, a hat. He came in, ill at ease, which he tried to cover by looking around with a pretense of being humorous. "What is eet, no Indian cloobs? I hear you were always schwinging Indian cloobs."

"I still schwing them, but not as much as I used to."

Billy sat down; his hand went into his pocket and out came a German pipe. He began to tamp in the tobacco with a stained finger. How well Griffith knew those wonderful hands, those hands which were always discolored by chemicals and developing fluids.

"I see you've got the same discolored hands," said Griffith lightly.

"It is zo. You see the bluish specks?"

"Yes."

"You put dem dere, Mr. Greeffith. When we make *The Birth* a bomb for de battle come so close it burn my handt."

They talked of the "old days." "I wish I could made *Rescue from an Eagle's Nest*," said Billy humorously. "Maybe I could have make de eagle look bigger!"

"How long is it we have been together, Billy?" Griffith asked as they talked.

"Dot is what I wish to speak of. I have count it oop andt it is sixteen year."

"Is it possible! Well, say, we've put some over home plate, haven't we?"

"It is zo. But mebbe it is no more."

"What do you mean, Billy?" asked Griffith, catching the serious note in Billy's voice.

So choked was Billy it was a moment before he could answer. "I am leaving you, Mr. Greeffith. I am to go where more money is."

"Listen, Billy," said Griffith, immensely concerned. "You wouldn't leave me. I can't get along without you."

Billy was touched. "It is the money. My family it is growing. I promise mine wife."

"Maybe I can arrange for you to get more money, Billy."

"I have promise."

"I'm going to Germany to make *Isn't Life Wonderful.* I want you to go along with me, Billy. You could jabber that language right back at them. Do you remember the trouble we had getting you into France to make *Hearts of the World?*"

"I laugh now, but I didn't den."

"Will you go with me, Billy?"

"I am sorry. I have promise."

They continued to talk, both sad that the old days were over. The two would have to go their different ways. How would each fare?

After Billy left, Griffith sat for some moments, reflecting on life, then turned back to his writing.

His dewy-eyed, golden-haired heroine was giving way to a quite different creature—the kind represented by Clara Bow, Mae West, Theda Bara. The simple cottage that his heroine, in his stories, had always inhabited was giving way to Malibu mansions. Worst of all the business office was calling for "commercial" pictures—pictures that would fit neatly into the weekly change of program and wouldn't cost too much. Griffith had no heart to make them. But whether he liked it or not, he must keep turning them out. How long would the demand last?

Griffith left July 4, 1924, for Germany with his two new stars, Carol Dempster and Neil Hamilton.

Isn't Life Wonderful was released in December of that year. The story dealt with displaced people in Europe trying to find new homes and to live.

The public had had enough of war and wanted no more of it. The picture was an artistic success, a financial failure.

Mutterings were coming from the exhibitors. They were booking the pictures because of his fabulous name, but his pictures were not filling the theaters. Had Griffith lost his touch?

A cold wind blew across him. A person he had watched with great interest was William S. Hart, who had the curious middle name of Surrey, and who was five years older than Griffith. Hart was born in Newburgh, New York, of parents almost as poverty-stricken as Griffith's. The Hart family had gone West, to Dakota Territory, and there young Hart had grown up. Later the family had to come back to Newburgh where Hart's father was the janitor of an apartment house. When young Hart was old enough to know what he wanted to do, he had become a Shakespearean actor. In 1914 he had gone into films, first as a "straight" actor, then as a Western. His success was amazing. No one could look down a pistol barrel with the steely eyes he could; in addition, he had a vertical crease between his eyes. When he tightened the crease, villains died in their tracks and innocent girls got safely back to the ranch house.

He knew enough about the West to insist that his pictures be true to life. One instance was that of swimming oxen across a river. For years directors had swum the oxen with their neck yokes on. Hart said this was utterly impossible and that the oxen would drown before they were halfway across. He was such a great star that he had his way: no neck yoke.

Other Western actors were coming along who did not try to be faithful to fact, but who played in the kind of romantic, glamorous, never-never-land pictures that the public liked.

Hart established the Good Bad Man—the man who was bad because he hadn't been treated right by society; or who was going to avenge the killing of his brother. The number of men roaming the West trying to find the skunk who had killed their brother was almost overwhelming.

Little by little Hart failed to be "box office." The crease was not bringing them in.

He began going down in 1920. He tried a comeback in 1922 and allowed himself to get mixed up in some bizarre publicity attempts. But his day was over. He made his last picture in 1925 —*Tumbleweeds*. So desperately eager was he for public attention that in 1927 he had a bronze statue of himself and his horse made by the sculptor C. C. Cristadora; it was called the "Range Rider of the Yellowstone." He himself paid for it and gave it to the city of Billings, Montana, where on a hill William S. Hart stands today looking out across the West he could not conquer.

His career had lasted eleven years.

Hart had been the greatest Western actor ever known. But now he was forgotten. What would happen to himself, Griffith asked? He would not be forgotten, he assured himself. A director was different.

A person he had little respect for was Tom Mix, who was born Thomas Edwin Mix, at Mix Run, Clearfield County, in the coal-mining section of western Pennsylvania. His father was the hostler to the rich man of the town; Tom, in reality, was born in the rich man's stable. He had run away from home, gone into the Spanish-American War where he had served with distinction. After a series of ups and downs he had gone to Guthrie, Oklahoma, where he was a bartender. Finally he had got into moving pictures and now, this year—the year William S. Hart was fading out, 1925—was making $17,000 a week. He had an elaborate home in Beverly Hills, a swimming pool, and an English butler.

Griffith studied this, too. What would happen to himself?

The stars he had made began joining other companies and working under other directors. New directors were coming in. The Germans were especially able; they employed devices he had invented and to them added their own. Among the new directors were Lubitsch, Seastrom, Von Stroheim—the latter had worked for him as an actor in *The Birth of a Nation.*

Griffith was growing desperate. He was living on the returns from *The Birth of a Nation.* The exhibitors were losing faith in him. He must do something. And then the idea came to him. He would make another spectacle like *The Birth of a Nation;* only this would be bigger. He would tell the story of the making of America—the birth of a whole nation, not just that of a section. His brain was on fire, as it had been when he had conceived other great pictures, and he set to work writing the story. He had long been interested in American history, and so, inspired, he began to write the story of America. One of the sequences would tell of Paul Revere's ride. When the time came for filming that part of the story, Griffith could not find a horse near Boston that suited him, so he got one in New York and had it brought to Boston in a van behind a car.

He engaged Carol Dempster and Neil Hamilton to play the love story that would hold history together. Finally he started the picture; again he was commanding great mobs of people—giving directions, telling them what to do.

Finally the picture—*America*—was completed and offered to the public in March 1924. It was a failure. In some places there were touches of greatness, but for the most part it was just plain dull. People didn't care whether Paul Revere got there or not.

Griffith was shocked. Why! he had a bigger and more important idea than he'd had in *The Birth of a Nation,* yet it was failing.

He'd make another picture; this time he'd win. But when he went to the bank, they refused to lend him money. Was it possible that the Great Griffith couldn't borrow enough to make a picture? It was possible, indeed.

He would have to give up his studio at Mamaroneck. A studio could not survive that made only one picture a year. A studio was like a factory: it had to be kept going at full capacity. So he gave up working for himself and got a job directing for Paramount.

Jazz was all the go. He would direct jazz. That was a long way from white rabbits, but he plunged into it. His jazz picture was a failure. The try showed that a person had to do the kind of picture that was deep in him, something he believed in, and which was not a faint copy of someone else. He still believed in a girl with dewy lips and starlit eyes, but there was no demand for that kind of girl.

A new star was in the sky—W. C. Fields. Griffith was given a story called *Sally of the Sawdust* with Fields, Carol Dempster, and Alfred Lunt. When the picture was previewed, Carol Dempster, so Broadway said, talked Griffith into cutting down Fields' role and building hers up. The company reshot several scenes; indeed, it spent $25,000, according to brother Albert, for that very purpose. When the picture was again assembled and released, August 1925, the reviewers looked on Carol with cold and aloof interest, but for Fields they got out their adjectives, saying, "Why isn't there more of Fields?" But Griffith, with his uncertain judgment of comedy, couldn't see this; he could see only the charming and delightful Carol.

So great was her hold on him, that he starred her in another picture—*That Royle Girl*—released in January 1926.

I asked Edwin Balmer if he had any memories of *That Royle Girl* and Griffith. He said:

"Griffith always liked to have a theme and the one in my book appealed to him. This is the theme: the idea that, out of the welter and strife of life in our big cities and from among people with little of the traditional good birth and breeding, there is arising as stanch and trustworthy an American as any descended from a passenger on the *Mayflower*.

"My best personal memory is not of Carol Dempster, but of W. C. Fields. It was his second appearance on the screen. He played the part of 'Dads' so well that his is the one characterization that stands out today in my mind. Oh yes! one other point. The advertisement in the Chicago papers said that the story had mystery, jazz, comedy, thrills, romance, drama, and a cyclone. I was stumped by the last named. There hadn't been a cyclone in my story. I rushed to the theater and there, in the story, was a wonderful cyclone. It had nothing to do with the story, but it was a rip-roaring cyclone. I felt proud of it."

The same thing happened. There was too much Fields, Carol Dempster said, and too little of herself. Griffith himself trimmed Fields down until he was as fleeting and shadowy as Tinker Bell. And again the critics looked at Carol and cheered for Fields. Still Griffith remained her champion.

Out of a clear sky came exceedingly good news.

William Randolph Hearst wanted to see him. The meeting was arranged by Walter Howey, then Hearst's favorite editor. Griffith met Howey, and after a little of this and a little of that, Griffith was ushered into the Presence. There they stood, the two men a bit alike in build and feature—Hearst with his hawklike expression and Griffith with his great beak of a nose. In backgrounds and tradition the two were wholly unlike. Hearst was the son of Harvard; Griffith hadn't gotten into high school. But here, for this moment, the two were equals.

The situation soon developed. Hearst had bought the motion-picture rights to the Barrie play *Quality Street* and wanted to star Marion Davies.

"I want you to direct it, Mr. Griffith, and I'm prepared to pay you ten thousand dollars a week and give you fifty-one per cent interest in the film."

Griffith could hardly believe his ears. Ten thousand dollars a week! Of course Linda would get 15 per cent, but a tidy sum would still be left. On top of the salary there was the division of profits.

It was a great, an exciting moment, but—

"I'm afraid I can't, Mr. Hearst. I have another commitment."

The other "commitment" was his word to Carol Dempster; he had promised her she would be the star in his next picture, and he would live up to his promise.

Finally the interview was over, and Griffith left.

The picture was directed by Sidney Franklin and was rated a success.

One day Carol Dempster approached Griffith as he was sitting in his director's chair filming a scene. Immediately he was all attention; he was puzzled why she had come, yet delighted to see her. She was always, he thought, doing the unexpected.

They talked a few moments, then she bent toward him and lowered her voice. "D. W., I have something to tell you. I hope you will take it right. I'm going to be married."

He tried not to show he was shocked, but a little of life seemed squeezed out of him.

She was, she continued, going to marry a broker.

She left almost as suddenly as she had come. He began again to direct the scene.

In all, he had her in twelve pictures. *Variety* said that he and the companies that financed these pictures spent $2,500,000 to make her a star.

At about this time a girl from Bellaire, a small town on Long Island, went with her mother to a charity bazaar at the Astor Hotel. It was a stuffy affair. People who had never seen each other before and hoped they would never see each other again talked energetically, as if enjoying every wonderful moment. The guest of honor was D. W. Griffith, the great director, the man everybody was talking about.

The girl was Evelyn Marjorie Baldwin.

As she was sitting there, Griffith walked across the floor, all eyes upon him. He had on a high collar, a long-tailed afternoon coat, and an Ascot tie, the very pink of male perfection. The women gathered around him, as bees around a honey jar.

In spite of the buzzing around him, Griffith's eyes fell on Evelyn and they lighted up, and well they might, for she was exceedingly nice-looking.

He stalked by her, looking intently at her as he did so, then turned and stalked back, his eyes again upon her, as a person, who has long been in prison, might gaze upon a sunset.

Turning, he came up and stood towering above her.

"You're Little Nell," he said, then turned and again took up his pacing.

At the far side of the room, he paused and his eyes again beheld the sunset. Coming back, he said, "You're Little Nell," then walked on again.

At last, by a miracle such as can happen only in a crowded bazaar, he managed to get a seat next to her.

He tried to talk to her, but earnest ladies came up and interrupted. Finally he said, "I guess you think this is a bit odd, and, for that matter, it is. I'm going to make Dickens' *Old Curiosity Shop* and I think you could play Little Nell."

"I'm not an actress," the astonished girl managed to say.

"That's a good sign. You haven't any preconceived ideas. I've taken a hundred who've never acted before and turned them into actresses."

He said, as they talked, that picture making was always on his mind, even in the throes of a public function.

When time came for the bazaar to break up, Griffith returned to the girl and her mother, and asked if he might call.

The girl, rather overwhelmed, said he could.

What a puzzling world he was moving in, Griffith thought. Once he had been sure of himself; had looked on himself as a genius. Now . . .

He was not so arrogant. Instead of wanting to attract attention, he began to evade it. He no longer strutted through the lobby of the Hotel Astor. His attitude was "he would show them," and he worked harder than ever at his writing. He sent a play to a manager; even his great name did nothing for it. Back it came. But he did not give up; some way or other he would yet be the American Ibsen.

He was more contemptuous than ever of motion pictures. Motion-picture theaters were still opiate palaces. Sometimes he would go to an opening; there he would sit, his cane in front of him, his hands clasped over its head, glaring at the screen. Sometimes, halfway through the picture, he would get up and walk out.

He tried again with *Drums of Love,* starring Lionel Barrymore and Mary Philbin, released in February 1928. It attracted little or no attention. He signed up two new stars and made *The Battle of the Sexes,* released in October that same year. It was a failure. He was growing desperate. Everything he turned his hand to failed.

From time to time he went to the movie theaters. They hadn't improved in ten years; more and more they were appealing to the simplest minds, he said. He'd make one more film, then get out of the miserable business. But he was still what was called a "big spender." He had an Italian car and a driver, and liked to sit in the back seat and drive down Broadway and through Times Square so people could see him and ask who he was.

Hollywood and picture making had undergone a radical change. At first a man could get a cast around him, rent space from a studio, get a small amount of money, and make a picture which would be released on a percentage basis. But all that had changed. Pictures had become "big business." It took a big studio to encompass a picture and it took a big organization to sell it; and mostly a picture was sold to the exhibitors before it was made. The small, so-called "independent" producer was being squeezed out. Pictures were becoming standardized. But Griffith was not one to make a run-of-the-mill product. He thought of the art rather than of how much the picture was going to cost, or how it was going to be sold. The business office said he was not "cooperative."

CHAPTER 14

TALKING PICTURES COME IN

A CHANGE CAME. FROM THE TIME HE HAD GOT
into pictures, pictures had been changing. First, there had been
the nickelodeons; then longer pictures had come. Then storytelling. The directors had, in reality, set up their cameras and
photographed a story as they would a stage play, with never
a change of position of the camera. Griffith righted all this;
the camera began to follow an actor like a farmer's dog following the farmer to town. The two-reel picture came in;
then came the mighty four-reeler—*Judith of Bethulia*. Then
came the day of the great outdoors spectacle. Griffith had introduced music; it was on recorded disks, but it sounded like
music. Also he had introduced an orchestra which was to sit
in a pit and play its head off.

The industry was drifting toward sound. Men shut away in
the Bell Laboratories were experimenting and tinkering, but
Hollywood paid little attention to this foolishness. Then came
August 6, 1926; the place the Manhattan Opera House, in
New York City. There was a flash, and on the screen appeared
Will H. Hays, so-called "czar" of the motion-picture industry.
He said he was introducing something that was going to revolutionize motion pictures—the Vitaphone. He talked from the
screen, but his voice came from a wax disk tucked away out of
sight. He was not exactly right, for the device revolutionized
nothing at all.

But something *did* revolutionize the screen. The year 1927 came and Warner Brothers prepared to exhibit a film in which there would be singing and talking, and the sound would be in the film itself and not on wax. It was to be called *The Jazz Singer* and the star was to be Al Jolson. In it Jolson said, "Come on, Ma, and listen to this"—the first words ever spoken on film. The result was electrifying—The Thing was talking.

In this picture Al Jolson, who was born in Russia, sang touchingly of his old southern mammy.

(When Warner Brothers had approached Jolson to do the picture, they said they would pay him in stock. Jolson was an old hand at pictures and astutely demanded cash. He was paid in cash, thus escaping becoming a rich stockholder.)

It was not long until there was a meeting of the Academy of Motion Picture Arts and Sciences. What was to be done with The Thing? D. W. Griffith got to his feet and spoke movingly, denouncing what he called "this new device" as a menace to a marvelous art. "It's a noisy monstrosity," he said feelingly. "It is a chattering horror. It will destroy all we have accomplished in creating a new art. It has no beauty—and beauty is the very basis of pictures. It has no soul. It mouths only gibberish and we should unite against it."

He sat down to tremendous applause.

They would all unite against it.

Meantime, Warner Brothers were moving ahead with the chattering horror. The picture earned them $3,000,000 and was such a tremendous success that Warners completely switched to sound and pretty soon were sitting on top of the Hollywood money.

One day Mary Pickford came to Griffith's studio—no curls now, but as lovely and appealing as ever. She was now the best-known woman in the world.

"I'm making my last silent picture," said Mary. "It's going to be released under the title *My Best Girl*."

This was something to think about. The idea lay in his mind like a seed in the soil.

He was engaged by United Artists to make another picture, this one to be called *Lady of the Pavements*. He was sinking into obscurity so fast that he had to get stars as best he could. None wanted to be with The Master. The ones he got, finally, were Lupe Velez and William Boyd—the latter was to become Hopalong Cassidy. He rushed the picture through, giving it none of the painstaking care he had used when he had been making his "big" pictures. When it was finished and he looked at it in the projection room, he said it was good enough for the kind of people who went to the movies. The picture was released in March 1929. It was a failure.

At last Griffith decided to make the Big Step. The other directors, he reasoned, would direct a picture as they had done when the movies had first come in, like a stage play. They would have the actors make full-arm gestures and exaggerated body movements. He would know something they didn't—and this was to keep as far away from the stage as possible. Movies, in that sense, had no relationship to the stage.

In writing his history of the War Between the States, he had become greatly interested in Abraham Lincoln who had been born not so far from where he himself had come into the world. In *The Birth of a Nation* he had shown the assassination. And now Griffith began to weigh the idea of telling the Lincoln story. Finally he began to write the story, as he had written so many for himself to produce. These were fine, exquisite moments, with no editor to send the story back.

At last it was done. But who could he get to play Lincoln?

At last he hit on Walter Huston, a Canadian; and on Una Merkel to play Ann Rutledge. Just the team.

He flew into his work with his old-time vigor. He'd soon be a director to reckon with.

The craze for talking pictures swept the country, like measles through a school. It was soon found that a poor talking picture would draw better than a good silent picture. One harried exhibitor said, "If you have a talking picture, you have to put up barricades to keep 'em out; if you are playing a silent picture, you have to tell 'em you've scattered diamonds under the seats."

It was not long until there was a series of billboards across the country with just two words—words that electrified the nation: GARBO TALKS.

All actors wanted to talk. But it was going to be rough on their egos. It was discovered that many of the actors, who looked regal on the screen, had voices like sissies; off the screen they went. On the other hand, it was also discovered that some of the chinless ones had fine, rich, impelling voices; onto the screen they went. John Gilbert had been the Great Lover of the Screen. He had made a million women discontented with their dull husbands. He spoke for the first time. A million women heard him and went cheerfully back to their husbands. But things did not go well with John Gilbert. His voice was thin, high-pitched, and squeaky. His contract was not renewed and he committed suicide.

Griffith found the new medium trickier than he had thought. Instead of simplifying problems, sound had increased them. Making a picture was just twice as difficult as it had been. All Hollywood was making talking pictures. Even Mack Sennett had his Bathing Beauties talking. It was soon discovered that their appeal was not in their pear-shaped tones. Charlie Chaplin himself was soon to talk; this proved to be a mistake. In fact, about the only actor in Hollywood who didn't talk was Lon Chaney, and he played deaf-and-dumb parts. And so ran the world away. Talk. Talk. Gabble. Gabble.

Talking pictures were no longer a novelty; in fact, some embittered souls said they wished the old silents would come back.

So poor were some of the talkies that a popular libel was "the smellies."

Now and then someone said the day would come when motion pictures would be made in color. That, of course, was foolish. Every industry has to have its crackpots.

It was at this time that his *Abraham Lincoln* was released. The exact date was August 24, 1930.

The exhibitors, who had expected another *The Birth of a Nation*, were disappointed; it was just a "programmer," with little southern appeal.

The critics regarded it as "just another picture." There were many fine Griffith touches, but as a whole it was down at the far end of the table. Compared to his great pictures, it was a failure.

It was just one year later that James Cagney, in a picture, squashed a grapefruit in a girl's face. This shocked the country; the pretty, demure Griffith girl was over the hill. The Sennett girl was packing 'em in.

These were hard days for the man who had once been The Master. A comfort and solace was Evelyn Baldwin, whom he had met that evening at the charity bazaar at the Hotel Astor. She was sweet and appealing, and was the first girl who interested him who was not an actress.

His old friends had become rich and famous. Douglas Fairbanks was popular wherever film would run through a projector. Charlie Chaplin had the world at his feet; every time he twirled his cane, people fell out of their seats. Thomas H. Ince was creeping up as Griffith's rival. Cecil B. De Mille was making "big" pictures. W. C. Fields was beginning to be talked about. Clara Bow, to whom Griffith had once refused a part, was the "It" girl and was making a million husbands look at the dirty dishes in the kitchen sink with a cold and critical eye.

Griffith got lower and lower in his mind. But he had no intention of giving up. He had once been supreme. He would be again.

His judgment of humor continued to be uncertain. Anita Loos wrote for him a story entitled *His Picture in the Paper*. It was directed by John Emerson and, finally, was finished. Griffith came to see the new baby.

The picture was run off in the projection room. He yawned his way through it. When it was finished he said, "It won't do. The laughs do not come from what the people do but from the lines that are flashed on the screen. People do not come to the theater to read. Put it on the shelf."

And there it lay, gathering dust. And then came a new situation. Roxy—S. L. Rothafel—had booked for his theater in New York a film version of *Macbeth* and had advertised it extensively. But the film didn't arrive. He waited till the last moment, looking wistfully into the street for a motorcycle, but none came. Only the audience.

At the last possible moment arrangements were made to show *His Picture in the Paper* in place of *Macbeth*. The film was taken from the shelf, the dust blown off, and inserted into the projector, Griffith groaning.

The audience began to pay attention. Soon it was laughing, such gales as hadn't been heard in a long time.

When the picture was finished and it was evident it was

going to be a substantial success, Griffith had a perplexed expression on his face.

"I can't understand why the audience laughed at what the characters said instead of what they did."

Griffith judgment of humor continued to be erratic. Once he said, "I want to study it more," and he did study it, fiercely and determinedly.

The picture itself marked the introduction of satire to films and was the picture that established Douglas Fairbanks.

Evelyn was a comfort, and to her he turned as a flower to the sun.

Most writers want people to read what they've written but Griffith had always been secretive about this. Now, as he came to know Evelyn better, he read his poetry to her and showed her his plays. She encouraged him. Here was someone who appreciated his talent.

Meantime he was being forced onto the shelf by the insistent demand for "standardized pictures"—pictures any director could make. Instead of being a towering figure, he was in competition with all the directors of Hollywood. He had once dominated Hollywood; now he was glad to get a picture to direct. He had been a big spender, a lavish tipper, but now his money was running downhill. And always there was the "settlement money" he had agreed, so long ago, to give Linda.

Once he had walked with the mighty, now he wanted to have as his friends lesser men who would look up to him and treat him with deference.

He gave up his Indian clubs. Too much trouble, he said. He made engagements but forgot them. When the disappointed person got in touch with him and reminded him what he had done, he was genuinely sorry and tried to make up for his remissness by being exceedingly kind.

In 1931 his luck changed. He was given the opportunity to direct a story written by Anita Loos and her husband John Emerson. It was to deal with prohibition. He was delighted. This was his old formula—a social problem handled in the terms of storytelling.

But he would have to put money of his own into it, the studio said. He hesitated, then finally agreed. Raising his share of the money was hard, but he managed it.

The first person he chose was Evelyn. Stars were becoming hard to get. He now got Hal Skelly, Zita Johann, and Helen Mack. The picture was made in the old Edison Studio in the Bronx—the very studio where he had fought the eagle twenty-four years ago.

The story pointed out the evils of Strong Drink. The United States was in the grip of a depression; soup lines were in every city. The people were thinking, not of strong drink, but of getting something to eat. Moreover, the story was laid on a depressing slum background. The picture was rushed through in three weeks.

Everything was against the success of the picture, but he believed in it. It would be his new start up the ladder.

The picture opened at the Rivoli Theatre, New York, December 10, 1931. It lasted two days.

The talk went up and down Broadway that The Master was through. But Broadway didn't know D. W. Griffith. He was not through; he would never be through. Once he had had three pictures running on Broadway at one time. He might never have that many again, but he would have a big and important one—something the newspapers would call a "typical Griffith production," as they had in the old days.

He began to count up the number of pictures he'd made. He was astonished he could not remember them all. But this was understandable, for in the Biograph days he had turned out two a week, mostly two-reelers; some he had not even gone to the theater to see before an audience. When his count was finished, he was astonished to find that he had made 427 pictures.

He'd make more.

Whatever was to happen, he had made seven great pictures:

TITLE	RELEASED
The Birth of a Nation	March 1915
Intolerance	September 1916
Hearts of the World	April 1918
Broken Blossoms	May 1919
Way Down East	September 1920
Orphans of the Storm	January 1922
Isn't Life Wonderful	December 1924

He was still living at the Hotel Astor. He came in quietly, spoke a few words to the desk clerk, then hastened to his room. Now he would have the chance to finish the plays he had been working on—especially *The Treadmill*, which dealt with the end of the human race.

He no longer went to The Players, the club that had once delighted him. He was more and more by himself. Now and then he dropped in to see a picture, but it was always so poor that he got up and left.

Then, out of a clear sky, came a triumph: he was voted the best film director for the year 1930–31. He was delighted; this would start him going again. But the word got out in

Hollywood that he was no longer "money," and nothing came of the honor.

He was like a caged tiger. His rivals were succeeding; he was accomplishing nothing. But he could find no opening. His money was growing lower.

He thought his presence might stir up interest, so he went to Hollywood. The papers reported his arrival, for he was a name that meant something. And usually he was good "copy." But he never gave out anything personal about himself. He had much to say about the industry and the stars he had worked with, nothing about his private life. He gave out that he was born in 1881 and told how he had been a reporter on the Louisville paper. He told an interviewer how he had once sold a poem to *Leslie's Weekly* for thirty-five dollars.

He hired a car, as he had done before, and went out to where he had made his mighty spectacle. The great walls had just recently been torn down; busses no longer brought tourists to gape. An apartment house was going up on the spot where the walls had once towered and where the plaster elephants had stood on their hind legs and held out their doubled-up forelegs; where the Nubian lions had roared, and where 16,000 extras had been served lunch at one time. He moved here and there, speaking to no one and asking no questions. After a time he got into his car and left for the Hotel Alexandria where he had lived during the Great Days.

He went, later, to see Mack Sennett. He was the same hearty, tobacco-chewing Mack Sennett. His studio was a beehive. Funny policemen rushed here and there; gay girls strolled the studio street, enjoying life.

"Come to my office," said Mack. They climbed a ladder to a strange-looking tower from which Mack could watch the operations of his madmen. He pushed a chair toward Griffith, put his heels on his desk, and began to chew, as a man does who enjoys himself.

They spoke briefly of the "old days"—the days of the fierce eagle and *The Curtain Pole*—but Mack saw that memories were painful, and dropped the subject.

"Come with me, Mr. Griffith, and I'll show you the new one." Even now, to the King of Comedy he was "Mr. Griffith."

Griffith spread his long frame over a couple of seats and stared in silence at the beautiful girls and beleaguered policemen.

"How do you like it?" Mack asked when the film finished.

"I guess you know what the public wants," he said, and Mack, seeing the anguish in the man's soul, said no more.

He left Hollywood and came back to New York. There had been no offer.

While he deliberated and turned this way and that, Mary Pickford, in 1933, appeared in her last motion picture—*Secrets*, with Leslie Howard. Her career was over; it had lasted twenty-four years. What about his own? Was it over?

In 1934 he was called to England by Twickenham Productions to do a talkie remake of *Broken Blossoms*, with the voices inserted into a sound track. He had the old silent picture run off two or three times, then sat in doubt, pondering what to do about it. Going to the company, he said, "It's a masterpiece as it is. I cannot add to it." The British company understood and the two parted amicably.

What to do now? No longer could he finance himself; motion pictures were "big business" and it took big companies to finance them. The little fellow was out.

With his world reputation, maybe he could get a chance to

direct a stage play. He called on managers, but they said that he knew only pictures and made him no offers.

However, an offer came from an unexpected source. Hinds', which dealt in beauty products, asked if he would do a radio program for them. He was hurt; talking on radio— what a comedown to a man who had revolutionized the screen. Radio! That silly gabbler. The thought came to him that this might keep him in the minds of the motion-picture officials, and so he agreed to do two weekly programs, each fifteen minutes, for thirty-nine weeks. In them he lived in the past, told stories of the "early days" in pictures. One talk dealt with the need of radio to find a personality who would be to radio what Mary Pickford had been to films.

He appeared for the thirty-nine weeks, as agreed.

There were no offers.

CHAPTER 15

HE RETURNS TO HOLLYWOOD WITH HIGH HONORS, BUT NO JOB

He was restless, this man who had been driving so hard all his life. Nothing to do. But something would open up.

While waiting, he went to Louisville. The *Courier-Journal* sent Francis E. Wylie to see Louisville's most distinguished son. He talked of the days when he had run the rope elevator and of the Meffert Stock Company. The reporter complimented him on his great pictures. Griffith grew silent, then finally said, half-choked: "I'd rather be a second-rate writer than a first-class director." Then he became silent again.

He went to the house in LaGrange where his mother had died eighteen years ago. It had been here that she had told him she wished he had become a preacher. What a fine southern woman she was, an aristocrat of the old days—days that would never return.

He went to the old farm; some of the rail fence still stood, but the house was gone, burned down. He started across the fields to the schoolhouse where he'd gone as a boy. He came to the creek where the willows had stood the morning he had seen the face of Christ. How long ago that seemed. Also how short. But it had influenced his life. Was that the reason he had put Christ in so many pictures?

The schoolhouse was no more. At last he left and returned over the path that he had just come along. Why! there were now no willows at all.

As a boy he had lived near the Floydsburg Cemetery, and now he went to the Duncan Memorial Chapel which had been built to honor the man whose name it bore. Griffith decided he would honor not only his father but also his family, and had built and set up in the cemetery a round stone seat as big as a dinner table, and on the rim of the circumference he had his family's record carved:

Honorable Salatheal Griffith, England and Virginia—father of Daniel Wetherby Griffith   Captain Daniel Wetherby Griffith, War of 1812   Colonel Jacob Wark Griffith, Mexican War, War of 1861   Presented by David Wark Griffith   VIRTUS OMNIA NOBILITAT

He went to Mount Tabor Cemetery to see the family plot, especially his father's grave. He was filled with emotion—his father who had really died for the South. He remembered what David Lloyd George had said about his father's military record, and a great pride moved through him. His father was a warrior and a God-fearing man. He would tell all who wished to know of his father's noble record for The Cause.

One genealogist was not enough; he set two to work looking up the family tree; one was to be in Washington, D.C., the other in the Filson Club, in Louisville. Each day he came proudly to the Filson Club library and pored over the records himself. He had a little gold pencil and jotted down information, bending almost tenderly over his notes. He had lost out in motion pictures, but his was a great family and he was proud to be a member of it.

When the record was completed, he had a granite stone set up at the head of his father's grave, and this tribute carved:

Twice elected to the House of Representatives. Served with Humphrey Marshall's First Kentucky Cavalry in the Mexican War. Commanded the first wagon train at this period to cross the Plains. The Lone Jack Unit, before arrival in California, suffered many attacks. Rescued a party of pioneers at Donner's Lake. Civil War—organized a company of Cavalry for the Confederate Service, for the First Kentucky Cavalry. In 1863 became Colonel of the First Regiment. Five times wounded, twice desperately, once at Hewey's Bridge, Alabama, May 8, 1862. Once after the capture of a 1,500 mule train, October 2, 1862. After a number of Confederates had been repulsed, General Wheeler asked Colonel Griffith to attack. Ten minutes later, the train had been captured. Suffering from previous wounds at the Battle of Charleston, Tenn., December 28, 1863, was unable to ride or walk. At a critical point in the battle, the First Kentucky was ordered by Col. Griffith to charge. Col. Griffith, not being able to lead his command on horseback, commandeered a horse and buggy, was helped in and led his Regiment to a victorious charge, cavalry probably never before having been led this way in all history.

He became more and more interested in Evelyn. Her father, a seafaring man, had been lost at sea, the body never recovered. Evelyn had been living with her mother at Bellaire, Long Island, and was little more than a schoolgirl when he had met her at the charity bazaar at the Hotel Astor, during which he had said she was "Little Nell." (He had not made the picture; a British version had been brought to the United States and he had dropped the idea of doing the story.) There was twenty-four years' difference in their ages; to him this seemed a small matter. She took up the study of shorthand and typing in order to be of help in his writing. He would, he said, dictate his stories to her.

As Evelyn meant more and more to him, he decided to sue for divorce from Linda. Evelyn, now quite efficient in stenography and typing, accompanied him to Louisville. The city again welcomed him. And there, the day before Christmas,

1935, he entered suit. The divorce was granted February 28, 1936, and he and Evelyn were married a few days later in the Brown Hotel in Louisville.

Hardly had he been married before an exceedingly good piece of news smiled on him: he was to be given the award of the Motion Picture Academy of Arts and Sciences—the highest honor Hollywood could bestow. He would now be able to get a job and again would be important.

He and Evelyn went to Hollywood and there, at the head table, the two sat surrounded by Hollywood's stars, many of whom he had made. When the time came, he was called on to speak. There he was!—the man who had influenced motion pictures more than anyone who had ever lived. The greats of Hollywood suddenly seemed to realize what he had done for them, and gave him a stirring ovation. He accepted the plaque with an appropriate speech. The audience applauded—it was thrilling to have the Great Man back.

He remained several days. But no offer came.

He heard of an opening in San Francisco and there he and Evelyn went, May 10. The town was excited—a movie was being made. He went to see the director—W. S. Van Dyke— the young man who had been a minor assistant in the filming of *Intolerance*. Now he was an important director, and was making *San Francisco*. He had 3,000 extras, a great number, the papers said.

Van Dyke spoke to The Master with great respect. "All I know I learned from you, Mr. Griffith." And now, for old times' sake, he asked Griffith if he would direct a scene.

Griffith was delighted. The world had changed. No mega- phone—a microphone, now. Not merely one Billy Bitzer, but three.

During the making of the scene Griffith walked with a

quick step and talked in a confident voice—again the man who had directed 16,000 extras from a balloon.

When he finished, he said, "I hope the scene turns out all right."

"It will," said Van Dyke.

And it did.

He returned to Hollywood. The papers carried the news, for he was important. But there were no offers. And he did not have enough money to finance a picture himself.

He took Evelyn to show her where he had made *Intolerance*. But the great set had been torn down; real-estate developers had been at work like beavers. However, it had been passed along to fame. In 1920 Columbia Pictures had made a documentary called *Screen Snap Shots*. A subtitle said, "He was the greatest director-producer of them all—the Genius of the Screen." In 1936 the company made another documentary based on the demolition of the great walls of Babylon. "Workmen crawl like pygmies over the hands and shoulders of the statue of Ishtar."

It was all very sad to look at, and, after a time, he and Evelyn left.

Later the two went to New York.

When Griffith got there, trouble was sitting on his doorstep: Linda had entered suit against him, claiming that his divorce was illegal and that he owed $50,000 in settlement money that he had agreed to in 1916. His answer was that he had paid her and her lawyers more than a million dollars. One statement came out of his heart: he said that Linda had falsely asserted she was the author of stories that he himself had written. This hurt him.

Suit and countersuit. It was all very unpleasant.

He had to go into hiding to keep from being served with

papers—humiliating to a proud man. He chose New Jersey and there secreted himself.

The Museum of Modern Art, in New York, had been established. Certainly motion pictures were an art, and D. W. Griffith was their world leader. So the Museum decided to give a reception to the man who had done so much for pictures, and a great, a happy time was planned for all. Would he be the guest of honor?

"What time of day would it be?" he asked guardedly when they telephoned.

"At four in the afternoon," said the Museum.

"I'm not free at that hour," he said.

"If we had it at eight in the evening, would you be free then?"

Griffith weighed this. "I think I could be. Have you a rear entrance?"

"Why, yes, we have," said the mystified Museum authority.

"I'd like to use that. People are always stopping me on the street and detaining me," said the modest man.

"It'll be at eight, then," said the Museum representative.

The evening came.

Griffith, with his collar turned up and his hat pulled low and wearing huge colored glasses, came in the back way. He scanned the faces of the guests. After a time he took off his wraps, displaying himself in elegant evening attire, and now, his mind free, he became the life of the party.

The evening was a tremendous success; everybody was delighted with him.

When the affair was over, he told his hosts good-by, put on his colored glasses, and crept silently into the night.

Life was moving along. Seemingly not much each day was happening, but when the days were added up, the change was startling. Was that the way of life?—a little each day, a great deal at the end of the year?

Now came unexpected good luck. At last he was freed from legal matters. He was overjoyed. He could be his own master. In 1938 he took Evelyn and went as fast as he could clop to Miami, Florida.

A reporter found him.

"I'm dead to the world of motion pictures," he said in his lofty way. "I'm an author," he added proudly. "I never liked the movies when I was working in them. Directing was just a job and I looked on it as temporary. My lifetime ambition has been to write, and now I can do it."

A strange quirk of psychology took place: the thing he had been trying to attain for years—a chance to write—was not so alluring as he had thought it would be. He began putting off, from day to day, his writing. He let little matters interfere.

Each morning he and Evelyn had breakfast together; he drank two cups of coffee, then began to dictate. After a time she handed him the pages; he made changes, passed them back, and again the typewriter clicked.

He would want to take a walk, or he would have a long-distance telephone call. When a telephone call came in, he would complain that he could not work because of the interruptions.

He sent his stories out, proudly signed with his full name. They came back. He worked on *The Treadmill*. It had a moving, an exciting idea; it would succeed. He sent it to managers. It came back.

It was not all bad news. *Liberty* accepted an article on the movies. It appeared June 17, 1939. He thought of his poem in *Leslie's Weekly* and spoke of it proudly.

He was not so thrilled now to see his article as he had been to see his poem, but, on the other hand, it was rewarding to have something in print in a magazine. It was not long before letters began to come in to him as a director—mostly wanting jobs. Ordinarily he did not pay any attention to letters that came to the studio, but this was different. As an author, he answered every one.

He became discontented with Miami; it did not have the right atmosphere for a writer, he said, and left.

The country became excited over a great super-picture— *Gone with the Wind*. Especially was Griffith intrigued, for it, too, was a story of the South and the War Between the States. But picture making had changed. To make *Gone with the Wind* had taken three years, instead of the seven months he had spent on *The Birth of a Nation*, and it had taken thirteen scenario writers, three directors, and had cost $4,000,000.

At last, in December 1939, came the opening date in Atlanta, Georgia, for *Gone with the Wind*. The mayor declared a three-day holiday and asked the men to raise sideburns, or imperials, and the women to appear in hoopskirts and the things that go with them. This they did; and again people marched down Peachtree Street, but this time no fiery crosses, no regalia, no pistols, no Ku Klux Klan. The world had changed, indeed.

One of the impressive scenes in the picture was the one in which the railroad depot was turned into a mighty hospital for the care of the wounded and dying. Griffith looked at it sourly.

"I got the same effect with a close-up of a few dead bodies."

He was eager to get news of his old associates. The Reverend Thomas Dixon was in Raleigh, North Carolina, in real estate, but was not doing well, the word was. The money he had made from *The Birth of a Nation* was getting away from him. A Democrat all his life, he had been forced to take a small appointed clerkship job from a Republican—a downright disgrace, so they said in Raleigh. Richard Barthelmess had gone to Southampton, Long Island, where he had bought a potato farm and where he was a favorite in the social set. Billy Bitzer was now working for a small salary for the Museum of Modern Art, New York, arranging and classifying the D. W. Griffith films. At his home, 109 West Sixtieth Street, New York, he had rigged up a laboratory where he was experimenting with the making and developing of film. The Gish sisters were appearing on the stage, having, for the most part, given up pictures. Lionel Barrymore was growling his way through film after film. Douglas Fairbanks was still leaping from place to place, but not quite so energetically. Alfred Lunt was now a Broadway favorite. The world was still mysteriously laughing at Mack Sennett's pretty girls and dumb policemen. Charlie Chaplin's tramp was becoming more and more unaccountably famous. W. C. Fields was moving on to greater and greater glory. Carol Dempster was forgotten. Bobby Harron had committed suicide. What a strange and puzzling world this was.

And then, as dazzling as a stroke of lightning, came exceedingly good news. Hal Roach wanted him to direct *1,000,000 B.C.* Griffith was delighted. Hollywood needed him.

Griffith thought of the picture he'd made so long ago—*Man's Ascent*. It had dealt with Darwin's theory. The business office had said it was doomed to failure—anything was doomed to failure that dealt with how men came into the world, except as related in the Bible. But he had gone ahead and made it and it had been an outstanding success—the exhibitors couldn't understand it.

Well, he would make a bigger and better one now. The two

men completed negotiations August 18, 1939. The film would say, "Produced by D. W. Griffith." The old days had returned. Why! this was just thirty-one years after *The Adventures of Dolly*. Motion pictures had come a long way since then. Had he?

When he arrived in Hollywood in 1940 he was a new man. Although he was sixty-five, he walked with a quick step. His old arrogance returned. He would whip the extras into shape. He would do a picture with a Message.

He soon discovered he was not the free agent he had believed himself to be. He must bow to the business office; he could do nothing without written authority—he who had once ridden so imperiously over the business office. In addition he discovered that his connection with the film was partly for publicity and that the business office did not take him seriously. It was a shock.

He resigned. The New York *Times*, April 20, 1940, reported that he had ordered his name removed from all credits.

A dinner was given him by the people of Hollywood who admired him so greatly. When his time came to speak, he got up and began, "Is there anybody here who would be willing to lend me ten dollars?" The people laughed; he was being at his humorous best, they said.

After dinner Mack Sennett came up and said, "You're still our head man, Mr. Griffith."

He remained in Hollywood a month longer, hoping something would "turn up," then he and Evelyn came back to New York.

He would not go into the picture palaces; they had silly and inconsequential pictures, he said, and used again the phrase that was coming oftener and oftener to his lips—"pictures are opiates for the masses."

He received a shock. Tom Mix was killed. Griffith had watched his career with a kind of lofty scorn. Mix could not act; he could only ride. But he had made money. Things, however, had not gone well with him. He had retired from the movies and had joined the Sells Floto Circus, a comedown. The circus idea had played out and he had joined the "Tom Mix Wild Animal Circus." He had given this up and gone into making serials, a still further comedown, Griffith believed. And now on this day—October 12, 1940—Mix had been killed in an automobile road accident near Florence, Arizona. When this had happened, Mix was on his way out of popular favor. Griffith studied this, too.

Not longer after this he read depressing news. Edwin S. Porter was the man who had made the immortal *The Great Train Robbery*, the first person in the world to tell a story on the screen. Yes, the very man who had given Griffith a job in *Rescued from an Eagle's Nest*. Porter had loved Broadway, which he had helped to make, and when his last days had come upon him, he had moved into the Hotel Taft, in the heart of the theatrical section, and there, in a silk dressing gown, had sat in an easy chair by a window so he could look down at the swarming crowds. Few of the people had ever heard of him. But that was all right; he'd had an exciting and successful life and there, in the hotel, the papers said, he had died April 30, 1941.

There suddenly swept down on the country a flood of pictures dealing with World War II. During the year 1942 sixty pictures were released that dealt in some way with war. Mostly they were pictures thrown together hastily and carried little meaning. Six companies rushed to the ex-Hays office to register the title *Remember Pearl Harbor*.

Some of the pictures Griffith liked. The best, he said, was

Sergeant York, the simple, faithful, touching portrayal of a young Kentucky boy, of a religious background, involved in a vast struggle which he didn't understand.

Others he liked were *Mrs. Miniver* and *Casablanca.* The poorest, he said, was *Mission to Moscow,* taken from a book signed by Joseph E. Davies, dealing with his days in Russia.

Griffith wanted to return to his early surroundings, where once he had felt secure, and with Evelyn once more went to Kentucky. This time he did not stop in Louisville but hastened to LaGrange. He moved into the house where his mother had told him she wished he had become a preacher. He would write now. Evelyn had brought her machine, but this was not enough —he hired another girl and now, with two secretaries, began to write. The big moment had come. The dream he had cherished for so many years was now an actuality.

He sent the stories out.

He had a box at the post office and himself went after the mail. When a story came back, he felt personally humiliated and tried to hide the rejection even from Evelyn.

He became discouraged; he said he must return to New York. As soon as he arrived in New York, he wanted to leave. He complained about not feeling well. He gave up his Indian clubs; he said he got enough exercise without flopping painted sticks around.

He began to pick out weaknesses and shortcomings in the motion-picture business. Many years before, he had been particularly shocked by the accusations made against Fatty Arbuckle. The comedian, in a night of debauchery, was accused of causing the death of a girl devoted to satisfying the wishes of men. There'd been nothing like this in the early days, he said. He regarded pictures sourly; rarely did he have a good word to say about any picture. "There hasn't been an advance in ten years," he said. "The things Billy and I invented are being proclaimed as new and revolutionary. It makes me sick at the stomach."

He began going to the theater alone. He would buy two seats, put his coat and hat on one, and sit through the whole performance without speaking to anyone. His presence would become known and people would come up, but he evaded them. The moment the curtain was down, he hastened out as if pressed by some great business matter.

His restless nature made it necessary for him to keep occupied. He had contributed his film and negatives to the Museum of Modern Art; the material had been catalogued. Billy Bitzer, when things were not going well for him, had worked on it and had saved many feet of precious negative. The work was done and was successful. But not to D. W. He insisted on going to the Museum and running the film backward and forward, as he had done with Jimmie Smith so many years ago. He would hold a strip of the ancient film before him, close one eye, and inspect the film. Then, picking up the scissors, he would snip out the part he didn't like. The Museum tried to get him not to make any changes, but their pleas meant nothing to him. Out would go another section of negative. He cut several hundred feet from *Intolerance*. "It's better now," he said when he finished.

Billy Bitzer sent word that he was ill, and would Mr. Griffith come to see him? Indeed, he would. Soon Griffith was at Billy's bedside in Saint Vincent's Hospital. Billy's hands were stained, as they always were—those amazing, square, blunt-fingered hands that had turned the crank on so many great pictures. And there were blue scars on them from powder burns made during the filming of *The Birth of a Nation*.

His savings were gone; he had lost everything he had, experimenting with colored motion pictures.

"How're you, Billy?" Griffith said, to be cheerful.

"Not well, not well. I don't know what is de matter mit me, but I have it all over."

The two talked of the early days—days when they had made world history. Billy managed a laugh. "You do not fight de eagle any more?" he said teasingly.

"You remember how you complained about the Clansmen's horses knocking your camera out of position? And how you never mentioned how close you came to being stomped to death by their hoofs? Do you remember that, Billy?"

"Yah. We was young den, Mr. Greeffith, is it not zo?"

"Pictures need something to build them up, they're so poor," said Griffith bitterly. He must cheer Billy up, not pull him down. "Tell me how you photographed William McKinley being notified on the lawn of his home that he had been nominated for President of the United States."

"You know dat ten t'ousand times I have tell you." But Billy did, at Griffith's urging, recount some of it over again.

"What're you working on now, Billy?"

"Motion pictures mit color."

"They'll never go, Billy. Color will take people's minds from the story."

"I don't t'ink it is zo."

"You didn't think I could make a four-reeler."

"I t'ink lots of dings wrong, but not dis one."

"You'll see, Billy."

At last Griffith left.

When Mary Pickford heard that Billy was ill at a charity hospital she arranged to have him moved to Saint Luke's where she paid his expenses from February 25, 1940, for the month he was there.

Billy Bitzer died April 29, 1944, and was buried in Cedar Grove Cemetery.

As the years had gone along, Griffith, from time to time, had heard from the Reverend Thomas Dixon. The news he had received was not good. And then, one day, when Griffith picked up the paper, there was the news that the author of *The Clansman* had died. The date was April 3, 1946, and the place was Raleigh, North Carolina, and there in Raleigh he was buried.

Griffith's friends and comrades of other days were going fast. He picked up the paper—bad news again: William S. Hart had died June 23, 1946—the great William S. Hart whose screen career had lasted only eleven years. After he was no longer wanted on the screen, he had busied himself writing boys' books—this man who once had electrified the world. In a few days Griffith saw something in the paper that made him blink—William S. Hart had left an estate of $1,170,000.

For some time things had not been going well between him and Evelyn. It had been a long time since he had looked at her and had exclaimed, "You're Little Nell!" and a long time since she had learned shorthand and typing. Then he had been planning to do *The Old Curiosity Shop*, with Evelyn as Little Nell, but a British version of the story had been released in this country, and he had given up the idea. But now conditions between him and Evelyn were different. She had been in *The Struggle*, the only picture she had appeared in that he had directed.

He had drawn into himself and sometimes read for half a day without speaking. Then suddenly he would rouse himself, determination would flood through him, and he would say he was going to make a new career for himself. But in this he was defeated before he began. He had no money to make a picture as he'd had in the old days; exhibitors looked on him with open suspicion. His last pictures hadn't made money; two days on Broadway for the last one. He wouldn't make a "commercial" picture, and that was what Big Business wanted—not an art picture that got fine reviews and no audiences. There was, however, one thing into which he could escape, and this was his writing. He would write a play that would in one great gesture establish him as an American playwright.

He went to Hollywood, hoping that one of the studios would send for him. Instead, on October 2, 1947, Evelyn filed papers for divorce. The reason she gave was that he was a "bachelor at heart." She asked for separate maintenance—bad news, for he was almost out of money.

CHAPTER 16

THE FORGOTTEN MAN

He moved into a side-street hotel in Hollywood. Theatrical trunks stood in the room and there were files for office papers. Battered, paint-scarred Indian clubs lay piled in the corner.

January 22, 1948, his birthday, came. Seventy-three—the true date he had hidden so long, but now he did not care. The important thing was to get on with his writing and he threw himself into it more earnestly than ever. He had so much to say, so little time to say it in. He would make the final revision of *The Treadmill*. Why! he had been working on that for fifty-one years. But that was all right. It took time to produce epochs.

Now and then doubt came and stood by his side. After all, was he gifted beyond others? He had contributed more to motion pictures than anybody who had ever lived, but he scorned them, and since he scorned them, he looked on himself as a failure.

A new idea developed. He would make a world-important picture about Christ and Napoleon. He would show a boy seeing the face of Christ in the willows, as he himself had done that morning on the way to school. He would have the thread run through the story, as the Rocking Mother had done in *Intolerance*. In the story he would contrast the ways of Christ and Napoleon and would show that the road of love was better than the road of blood. It was a great, a stirring, an important idea. It would be seventy-two reels long and would run for eight hours; audiences would have to go for three evenings to see it all. But they would go willingly—even eagerly—for it would deal with their souls and why they, themselves, were on this planet. From the tremendous profits he would have money enough to produce *The Treadmill*. He threw himself into the scenario, writing till dawn, as he had done so many times before. Now that he had the story, who would produce it? He did not have enough money; the studios looked on him as a ghostly figure out of the past.

He felt sensitive about this, and took umbrage easily. Men who had claimed him as friend found him hard to get along with. He kept more and more to himself. His tall, erect figure, with a big flopping hat, walked along the street—the street where once he had attracted so much attention. A new generation, however, had come along. He was out of the minds of the old stars and they paid little attention to him, and he was too proud to make advances. He became the Forgotten Man of Hollywood.

He let his letters accumulate without opening them, nor did he open telegrams or answer telephone calls. Once he had liked to go into the dining room of a hotel, for there had always been a flutter that the great director had come and could be seen by anyone who wished, but now he had his meals served in his room and ate alone and in embittered silence.

Reporters tried to interview him, but he would not see them. Finally, however, Ezra Goodman, representing *P.M.*, a New York paper, did get to see him. Griffith talked of how wide his reading was and how much he had read during his lifetime and how well he had remembered it. He spoke of the great new film he was going to direct and of *The Treadmill*. He said there had been no improvement in motion pictures in ten years and that forty years earlier he had made movies from poems and that no one would dare do that today. He spoke of *Pippa Passes* and proudly told how it had been reviewed by the New York *Times*.

His mind went back, oftener and oftener, to the people he had known in the early days: Edwin S. Porter, "Mr. Mc-Cutcheon," as he called him, Billy Bitzer, Mack Sennett, Mary Pickford, the Gish sisters, the ill-fated Bobby Harron, who had committed suicide. Each night he got out his papers and manuscripts and pored over them, making notes, now and then, with his little gold pencil.

He began to complain about "not feeling up to par"; it was the summer heat, he said, for July was upon him. His head "didn't feel right."

He had relatives in Santa Ana, near Los Angeles, and they came to see him. He seemed to want to have his family around him. Some of his nieces and nephews had never seen Crestwood, nor LaGrange; they had missed a great deal, he said; it was where their family had come from. He spoke of the old farm and of the death of his father from the five wounds he had received in the War Between the States. He spoke of his sister Mattie who had read to him stories of the days of old, and who had given him what little education he had. He spoke of the Meffert Stock Company and of Adolph Lestina who had told him that to be a playwright one first had to be an actor. He spoke of the way *The Birth of a Nation* had been received and how people had denounced him.

A brain hemorrhage developed. He died in the Temple Hospital at eight twenty-four on the morning of July 23, 1948.

He had not made a picture in sixteen years and many of the stars did not know that he was still living. They were saddened, they said, that the greatest director of all had died in obscurity and poverty. One paper ran the headline Aged Film Man Passes, and two paragraphs dealing with his career and a mention of what the paper called "the controversial picture" *The Birth of a Nation*.

The press associations got out obituary releases; most of them were wrong, for they were based on the misinformation that, over the years, had gone into the newspaper files.

Personal Memory, from Mae Marsh:

During his last days, he walked up and down the streets, a lone, solitary figure. He was acknowledged to be the greatest director who had ever lived, yet no one gave him a chance to direct. With John Ford I went to the funeral parlor where the body lay in state. The attendant told us that only four persons had come to pay their respects; one of them was Cecil B. De Mille. But next day, at the funeral, matters were different. The story was in the papers, and photographers would be present. The picture people came trooping.

His funeral was a perfunctory one—for Hollywood. Services were held the next day in the Masonic Temple. A tribute was paid by Charles Bracken, representing the Academy of Motion Picture Arts and Sciences, and a eulogy was delivered by Donald Crisp who had played General Grant in *The Birth of a Nation*. He lamented the fact that Hollywood had been cold to The Master and that Griffith had "beat against the doors of Hollywood," and that the doors had not opened. The honorary pallbearers were Lionel Barrymore, John Ford, Samuel Goldwyn, Richard Barthelmess, Monte Blue, Charles Chaplin, Cecil B. De Mille, Sid Grauman, Jean Hersholt, Walter Huston, Jesse L. Lasky, Louis B. Mayer, Hal Roach, Mack Sennett, and Adolph Zukor.

Lionel Barrymore, in speaking to one of the other mourners, gave the most personal touch. He said, "A gold monument should be erected at the corner of Vine Street and Hollywood Boulevard to D. W. Griffith, Hollywood's greatest."

The body was flown back to Kentucky and taken to Mount Tabor Cemetery and there he was buried within two miles of where he had been born.

Two years later Hollywood wanted to express its memory a little more feelingly than it had done, so through the efforts of the Screen Directors' Guild the body was taken up and moved about two hundred feet to a new grave where a stone was set in place over the grave, with a symbol at each end of the Screen Directors' Guild. Three of his stars loved him enough to come. They were Mary Pickford, Lillian Gish, and Richard Barthelmess; also present was Al Rogell representing the Guild. His widow, Evelyn Griffith, was also there. Fence rails were taken from the old farm and placed around the grave, and there they are today, very fitting and appropriate.

On top of the gravestone is carved:

DAVID WARK GRIFFITH
Born Crestwood, Kentucky, January 22, 1875
Died Hollywood, California, July 23, 1948

As I write, two immediate members of his family still live, and I again want to thank them for the great help they've been to me. His brother Albert L. Griffith lives at 325 West Avenue, Medina, New York. His widow, Mrs. Evelyn M. B. Griffith, lives at 535 East Fourteenth Street, New York. He has six relatives living in Oldham and Jefferson counties, Kentucky, and he has eight relatives living in or near Los Angeles.

The inventory shows that he left a gross estate of $25,039.97. There were many bills which he had run up the last few months. He mentioned ten people in his will, all relatives; the money that was left was divided among them.

As I finish this story, I think to myself: What will be his place in history? Will he continue to be the Forgotten Man of the entertainment industry? Will greater figures appear and stalk across the entertainment stage? I doubt it. And, some way or other, I hope there won't. He came at the very birth of a new and mighty art. It can almost be said that he made an art.

There is something touching and poignant about a man who yearns to do something and fails—and then, in a kind of I'll-show-you way, makes a commanding success of something he secretly looks down on. It has, it seems to me, the elements of the Greek theory of drama: that every man has within him seeds that make him and seeds that destroy him—sometimes the same seeds.